Collins

KS3
Science
Year 8

T0321489

Ian Honeysett, Sam Holyman
and Lynn Pharaoh

How to use this book

Each Year 8 topic is presented on a two-page spread

Organise your knowledge with concise explanations and examples

Key points highlight fundamental ideas

Test your retrieval skills by trying the accompanying questions for the topic

Mixed questions further test retrieval skills after all topics have been covered

Scientific skills section provides further knowledge and explanations of scientific ideas and investigative skills

Answers are provided to all questions at the back of the book

ACKNOWLEDGEMENTS

The authors and publisher are grateful to the copyright holders for permission to use quoted materials and images.

Every effort has been made to trace copyright holders and obtain their permission for the use of copyright material. The authors and publisher will gladly receive information enabling them to rectify any error or omission in subsequent editions. All facts are correct at time of going to press.

All images ©Shutterstock and HarperCollins*Publishers*

Published by Collins
An imprint of HarperCollins*Publishers* Limited
1 London Bridge Street
London SE1 9GF

HarperCollins*Publishers*
Macken House, 39/40 Mayor Street Upper,
Dublin 1, D01 C9W8, Ireland

© HarperCollins*Publishers* Limited 2023

ISBN 9780008598686

First published 2023

10 9 8 7 6 5 4

British Library Cataloguing in Publication Data.

A CIP record of this book is available from the British Library.

Authors: Ian Honeysett, Sam Holyman and Lynn Pharaoh
Publisher: Clare Souza
Commissioning: Richard Toms
Project Management: Katie Galloway
Inside Concept Design: Ian Wrigley
Layout: Rose & Thorn Creative Services Ltd
Cover Design: Sarah Duxbury
Production: Emma Wood
Printed and bound in the UK

MIX
Paper | Supporting responsible forestry
FSC www.fsc.org
FSC™ C007454

This book contains FSC™ certified paper and other controlled sources to ensure responsible forest management.

For more information visit:
www.harpercollins.co.uk/green

Contents

1 Biology

What is the human skeleton? 4
What are joints? 6
What are muscles? 8
How do we get energy? 10
How do plants get their energy? 12
What are body systems? 14
What is anaerobic respiration? 16
Why are plants important? 18
What is photosynthesis? 20
How can we investigate photosynthesis? 22
Why do plants need minerals? 24
What is a food web? 26
What is interdependence? 28

2 Chemistry

What is the particle model? 30
What is changing state? 32
How can the particle model be used to explain properties? 34
What is density? 36
What is concentration? 38
What is diffusion? 40
What are the properties of mixtures? 42
What are the differences between acids, alkalis, bases and neutral chemicals? 44
What is neutralisation? 46
What happens when acids react? 48
What is combustion? 50

3 Physics

What is static charge? 52
How does gravity change in different parts of space? 54
What causes pressure on the surface of a solid? 56
What causes pressure in a liquid? 58
What causes pressure in a gas? 60
What are magnets? 62
What are the different types of magnet? 64
How can electromagnets be used? 66
What is the motor effect? 68
What is an electric circuit? 70
How can we investigate electrical resistance in a circuit? 72

Mixed questions 74

Scientific skills 78

Answers 82

1 What is the human skeleton?

Main bones of the skeleton

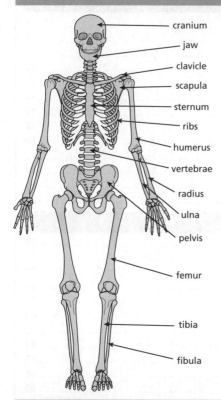

cranium
jaw
clavicle
scapula
sternum
ribs
humerus
vertebrae
radius
ulna
pelvis
femur
tibia
fibula

There are 206 different bones in the human skeleton:
- the **cranium** (skull) protects the brain and is made up of a number of bones that are fused together
- the **vertebrae** are lots of small bones that make up the **vertebral column** (backbone) and protect the spinal cord
- the arms have one long bone called the **humerus** and two smaller bones called the **radius** and **ulna**
- the leg has the same pattern of bones as the arm, with a long **femur** bone and the **tibia** and **fibula**
- the hands and feet are made of many small bones.

Functions of the skeleton

The human skeleton has four main functions:
- it **supports** the body, holding it upright
- it **protects** delicate organs, such as the brain and spinal cord
- it allows **movement** through the actions of the arms and legs
- it **produces blood cells** in the bone marrow of the bones.

Bones and bone damage

Bones that make up the skeleton need to be strong but slightly flexible. If they were too brittle, then they would break.
- Most of the bone is made of hard minerals containing **calcium**.
- They also contain fibres of **protein** that make them flexible.

Scientists can use measurements from individual bones of the arm or leg to estimate the height of the person, e.g.
height in cm = (length of femur in cm x 2.6) + 65

Although bones are strong, they can break or fracture. Breaks and fractures can be investigated using X-ray images of the damaged area. The fractures can then be treated in different ways:
- by making a plaster cast to hold the bones together so that they can repair themselves
- by inserting metal pins or plates to hold the bones together.

As we get older our bones become less dense and more likely to fracture. This is called osteoporosis.

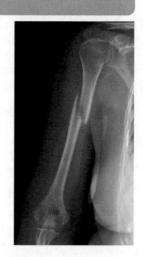

① What is the human skeleton?

Main bones of the skeleton

1 Write down the name of each of these bones. Use the diagram of the human skeleton on the opposite page to help you if needed.

a) The bone that protects the brain

b) The bones that surround the lungs

c) The largest bone in the leg

d) The two bones in the arm between the humerus and the hand

Functions of the skeleton

2 Which bones in the skeleton protect the spinal cord?

3 What is the function of the bone marrow?

Bones and bone damage

4 What makes human bones slightly flexible?

5 The photograph shows damage to a bone in a person's leg.

a) What type of machine has been used to take this photograph?

b) What is the name of the bone in the leg that has been broken?

c) Write down **two** ways in which this break could be treated.

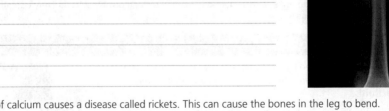

6 Lack of calcium causes a disease called rickets. This can cause the bones in the leg to bend. Explain why.

(1) What are joints?

Types of joints

Wherever two bones meet, they form a **joint**. Sometimes the joint does not allow the bones to move. These are called **fixed joints**. Examples are the joints between the bones of the cranium.

Other joints allow the bones to move. There are three main types of **moveable joints**:

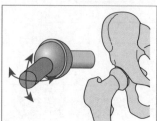 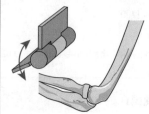 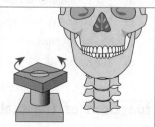

Ball and socket joints	**Hinge joints**	**Pivot joints**
They allow almost 360-degree movement. Examples are found at the hip and the shoulder.	They allow 180-degree movement, like a door hinge. Examples are found at the knee and the elbow.	They allow limited movement as two bones rotate. Examples are found between the vertebrae in the neck.

Structure of joints

Moveable joints contain different tissues to allow the two bones to move smoothly:

- **cartilage** is a smooth rubbery substance that coats the ends of the bones to absorb shock and stop the bones rubbing together
- the joint is filled with a slimy liquid called **synovial fluid**, which reduces friction between the bones
- **ligaments** are elastic tissues that hold bones together to prevent the joint dislocating.

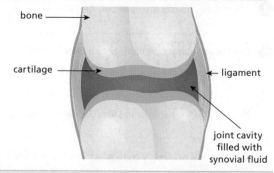

bone

cartilage

ligament

joint cavity filled with synovial fluid

It is important that ligaments at the knee and hip are strong but elastic, so they can absorb shock when a person runs.

Problems with joints

Our joints can be damaged by wear and tear over many years. The cartilage can wear away and the bones can rub together. This is called **arthritis**.

Sometimes the ball of the pelvis can be affected by arthritis or may break off if the bone is weak. This means a person may need an artificial hip joint.

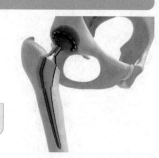

Arthritis is very painful because the bones that are damaged are living tissues and contain nerves.

What are joints?

Types of joints

1 Look at the diagram of the human skeleton.

Write down the letter that labels the position of each of these joints:

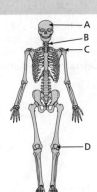

A
B
C

a) a fixed joint ☐

b) a hinge joint ☐

c) a ball and socket joint ☐

d) a pivot joint ☐

D

2 Which type of moveable joint allows the most movement?

....

Structure of joints

3 **a)** What is the name of the substance that coats the ends of bones?

....

b) What is the function of this substance?

....

....

4 **a)** Which tissue prevents joints dislocating?

....

b) Why is it important that this tissue is elastic?

....

5 What is the name of the liquid in joints that reduces friction between the bones?

....

Problems with joints

6 What causes arthritis?

....

....

7 Artificial hip joints contain metal parts.

Suggest which properties are important when choosing the type of metal used to make artificial joints.

....

....

....

1 What are muscles?

How do muscles work?

There are three types of muscle in the human body:
- **cardiac muscle** is found in the heart and it contracts to pump blood
- **smooth muscle** is found in the blood vessels, the digestive system and the uterus
- **skeletal muscle** is attached to the skeleton and allows us to move.

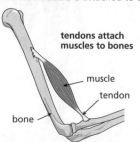

tendons attach muscles to bones

muscle

tendon

bone

Skeletal muscle is the only type of muscle that can be consciously made to contract. This happens when nerve impulses from the brain reach the muscle.

Skeletal muscle makes up the muscles that move our bones. They are attached by strong **tendons**.
When the muscles contract, the bones move because the joints act as pivots.

Working in pairs

To allow our body to move, muscles often work in pairs.
- When one muscle contracts (such as the **biceps** in the arm) it gets shorter. This pulls on the bone and moves it.
- The other member of the pair (which is the **triceps** in the arm) will be stretched.
- If the bone needs to be moved back, then the triceps will contract and the biceps relaxes.

Pairs of muscles that work in this way are called **antagonistic muscles**.

Muscles can only contract to pull on bones; they cannot push. That is why they have to be arranged in **antagonistic pairs**.

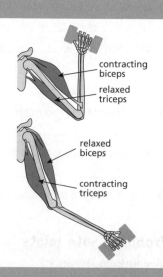

contracting biceps

relaxed triceps

relaxed biceps

contracting triceps

Measuring muscle strength

Sportspeople often want to know if their muscles are getting stronger. They can test this by measuring how much force a muscle can develop. The unit for force is **newtons (N)**.

For example, the muscles that move the fingers can be tested using a machine that measures the strength of the grip. Studies of muscle strength are examples of **biomechanics**.

Some sportspeople take illegal drugs called anabolic steroids to try to increase their muscle strength. These drugs can have dangerous side effects.

① What are muscles?

How do muscles work?

1 Which organ in the body contains cardiac muscle?

2 What is the function of tendons in the body?

3 What makes skeletal muscles contract?

4 What is the function of joints in movement?

Working in pairs

5 The diagram shows some of the muscles in the arm.

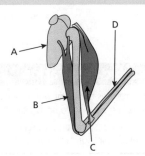

a) Which letter on the diagram labels:

i) the biceps? ☐

ii) the triceps? ☐

b) What would happen to the arm if muscle B contracts?

6 What name is given to muscles that work in pairs?

7 Explain why muscles often need to work in pairs.

Measuring muscle strength

8 Put a ⟨circle⟩ around the figure that could be a measure of muscle force.

| 100cm | 100J | 100N | 100W |

9 Why do some sportspeople take anabolic steroids?

1 How do we get energy?

Why do we need energy?

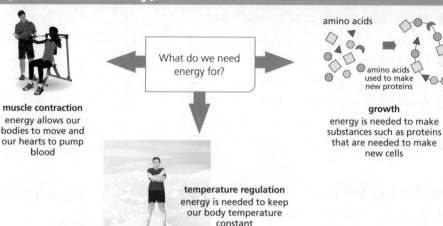

muscle contraction
energy allows our bodies to move and our hearts to pump blood

What do we need energy for?

growth
energy is needed to make substances such as proteins that are needed to make new cells

amino acids

amino acids used to make new proteins

temperature regulation
energy is needed to keep our body temperature constant

Aerobic respiration

Food provides the body with chemical energy. When food is digested, nutrients such as glucose are carried in the blood to body cells. Respiration then releases the energy in glucose to be used by cells.

The type of respiration that releases the most energy uses oxygen. This is called **aerobic respiration**. Aerobic respiration is shown in this equation:

glucose **+** oxygen $\longrightarrow$ carbon dioxide **+** water **+** energy released

> Remember to say that energy is **released** by respiration and not **made**.

Oxygen is obtained from air in the lungs. Carbon dioxide and water are waste products and are lost from the lungs.

Where does respiration happen?

Aerobic respiration happens in small structures called **mitochondria**, which are scattered throughout the cytoplasm of cells. The diagram shows the structure of mitochondria:

- they are surrounded by two membranes
- the inner membrane is folded so it has a larger surface on which respiration takes place
- the inner matrix contains enzymes needed for the reactions.

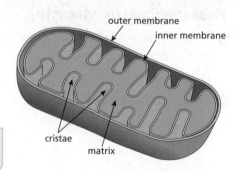

outer membrane

inner membrane

cristae

matrix

> Remember that both animal and plant cells have mitochondria, so aerobic respiration happens in both animals and plants.

RETRIEVE

1 How do we get energy?

Why do we need energy?

1 Which process requires energy and allows the body to move?

....

2 Energy is needed to make proteins. What are proteins made from?

....

3 Explain why the heart needs energy.

....

....

Aerobic respiration

4 Complete the equation for aerobic respiration.

glucose + ... → .... + ...

5 Describe how the oxygen needed for respiration reaches body cells.

....

....

6 A student wrote this sentence about how cells obtain their energy:

Energy is made in cells by the process of breathing.

Rewrite this sentence, correcting the mistakes that the student has made.

....

....

7 What are the waste products of aerobic respiration?

....

Where does respiration happen?

8 Mitochondria are structures that are adapted for aerobic respiration.

Explain how these parts of mitochondria are adapted:

a) inner membrane ....

....

b) matrix ....

....

1 How do plants get their energy?

What is photosynthesis?

Although they do not move, plants still need energy for different processes. As in animals, this energy comes from respiration. However, plants do not eat to get the glucose for respiration. They make their own glucose using **photosynthesis**.

Photosynthesis uses the energy from sunlight to make glucose from carbon dioxide and water.

$$\text{carbon dioxide} + \text{water} \xrightarrow{\text{light energy}} \text{glucose} + \text{oxygen}$$

How do plants transport substances?

Plants need to get carbon dioxide from the air, and water from the soil, into their leaves for photosynthesis. They also need to transport the sugar that is made to all the cells of the plant for respiration or to be used in growth.

	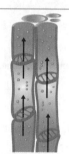	
Carbon dioxide diffuses into the leaves through tiny pores called **stomata**.	Water is drawn up from the roots to the leaves through long, thin tubes called **xylem vessels**.	Sugar is transported from the leaves to all parts of the plant through **phloem sieve tubes**.

The cells that make up stomata, xylem vessels and phloem sieve tubes are all specialised for their jobs.

Photosynthesis and respiration in plants

Plants will photosynthesise during the day when it is light, but they respire day and night.

If there is any unused glucose, it is converted to **starch** and stored.

You can test to see if there is starch stored in a leaf by using iodine solution:
- First, boil the leaf in ethanol to kill it and remove the green colour.
- Rinse in warm water to soften the leaf.
- Pour iodine solution over the leaf and if it turns blue–black, starch is present.

leaf after extracting green colour

leaf after iodine is added

If a plant is kept in the light, then the leaves will turn black when tested for starch. If the plant is put in the dark for 24 hours, then the starch test is negative. This is because it has used up the starch in respiration.

1 How do plants get their energy?

What is photosynthesis?

1 Which of the following are products of photosynthesis? Tick the **two** correct answers.

glucose ☐   water ☐   carbon dioxide ☐   light ☐   oxygen ☐

2 Where does the energy for photosynthesis come from?

_____

How do plants transport substances?

3 Complete these sentences about photosynthesis and transport in plants.

To allow plants to photosynthesise, they need _____ gas from the air.

This gas enters leaves through small pores called _____. Plants also need water,

which is taken up by roots from the _____. The water passes up to the leaves in long,

thin tubes called _____.

4 What is the function of phloem sieve tubes in plants?

_____

_____

Photosynthesis and respiration in plants

5 When do these processes happen in plants?

a) photosynthesis _____

b) respiration _____

6 A student plans a method to test a leaf to see if it contains starch.

This is their plan:
- **Step 1:** boil a leaf in ethanol
- **Step 2:** rinse the leaf in warm water
- **Step 3:** pour Benedict's solution over the leaf and if it turns red, starch is present.

a) What is the purpose of step 1?

_____

b) Explain why, in step 1, the leaf should be boiled in a water bath after turning out the Bunsen burner.

_____

_____

c) Step 3 in the student's method contains two mistakes.

Rewrite step 3, correcting the mistakes.

_____

_____

Different body systems

The human body contains eleven different systems. A system is made up of organs that work together to perform important functions needed for the body to survive.

Three of these systems are the **digestive system**, the **breathing system** and the **circulatory system**.

In the circulatory system, blood is pumped by the heart into **arteries** and comes back to the heart in **veins**.

The circulatory system

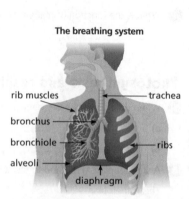

main vein from the head and arms

main artery to the head and arms

artery to the lungs

veins from the lungs

main vein from the digestive system and other organs

heart

main artery to the digestive system and other organs

The digestive system

mouth
salivary gland
oesophagus

pancreas
stomach
large intestine
small intestine
appendix
anus

The breathing system

rib muscles
trachea
bronchus
bronchiole
ribs
alveoli
diaphragm

Working together

The digestive system, the breathing system and the circulatory system all work together to allow the cells of the body to respire:
- the digestive system supplies glucose
- the breathing system supplies oxygen and gets rid of carbon dioxide
- the circulatory system transports these substances to and from the cells.

If any of these systems are not working properly, respiration may stop and this can cause death.

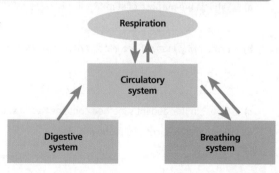

Respiration

Circulatory system

Digestive system

Breathing system

1 What are body systems?

Different body systems

1 Which organ in the circulatory system pumps blood?

_____

2 Which type of blood vessel carries blood from the heart to the lungs?

_____

3 Which type of blood vessel carries blood from the head to the heart?

_____

4 In which part of the digestive system does food enter the bloodstream?

_____

5 Which glands release enzymes into the mouth?

_____

6 Write down the names of **three** different tubes in the breathing system.

_____

_____

_____

Working together

7 Complete these sentences about the digestive system and the breathing system.

The digestive system contains a sugar called _____ that is needed for respiration.

The breathing system provides the gas _____, which passes into the bloodstream

in the lungs. This happens in small air sacs called _____. Respiration produces the gas

_____, which passes into the air in the lungs.

8 When somebody has an asthma attack, the bronchioles taking air to the lungs get narrower.

Explain why this might reduce the energy available in body cells.

_____

_____

_____

_____

What is anaerobic respiration?

When and where does anaerobic respiration happen?

Sometimes there is not enough oxygen available for aerobic respiration to happen. So that they can still release energy, cells switch to **anaerobic respiration**.

Compared with aerobic respiration, anaerobic respiration:

- does not need oxygen
- releases less energy
- takes place in the cytoplasm not the mitochondria
- makes **lactic acid** rather than carbon dioxide and water.

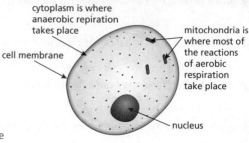

cytoplasm is where anaerobic repiration takes place

cell membrane

mitochondria is where most of the reactions of aerobic respiration take place

nucleus

Anaerobic respiration in animal cells is shown in this equation:

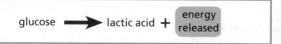

glucose ⟶ lactic acid + energy released

> Both anaerobic and aerobic respiration are controlled by enzymes. Enzymes are protein molecules that speed up the rate of biological reactions.

Anaerobic respiration in yeast

Yeast cells also respire anaerobically but the reaction is different to anaerobic respiration in animal cells.

Anaerobic respiration in yeast is shown in this equation:

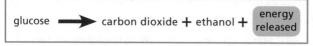

glucose ⟶ carbon dioxide + ethanol + energy released

> Yeast cells do not make lactic acid but produce **ethanol** (alcohol) and carbon dioxide instead.

Anaerobic respiration in yeast is often called **fermentation**.

This is used in the brewing industry to make alcoholic drinks and in baking to make bread.

> The carbon dioxide produced by yeast makes beer and cider fizzy, and also makes bread rise.

Measuring the rate of fermentation

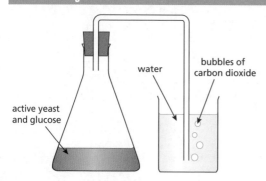

water

bubbles of carbon dioxide

active yeast and glucose

It is possible to show that fermentation makes carbon dioxide by bubbling the gas made through limewater, which will turn milky.

The rate of fermentation can be measured by counting the number of carbon dioxide bubbles given off in a minute.

The effect of changing the temperature or the concentration of glucose can be investigated.

What is anaerobic respiration?

When and where does anaerobic respiration happen?

1 Put ticks and crosses in this table to compare aerobic and anaerobic respiration in animal cells.
The first row has been done for you.

	Aerobic respiration	Anaerobic respiration
Does it release energy?	✓	✓
Does it use oxygen?		
Does it use glucose?		
Does it make lactic acid?		
Does it happen in mitochondria?		

2 Anaerobic respiration is controlled by enzymes. What are enzymes?

....

....

Anaerobic respiration in yeast

3 Complete the word equation for anaerobic respiration in yeast.

glucose → .... + ... + energy released

4 Complete these sentences about anaerobic respiration in yeast.

Anaerobic respiration in yeast cells is also called .... It is used in bread making as

the .... gas that is produced makes the bread rise.

Measuring the rate of fermentation

5 What effect does carbon dioxide have on limewater?

....

6 A student wants to measure the rate of fermentation in yeast.
They modify the apparatus shown on page 16.

This diagram shows the new apparatus.

a) Explain why the student puts a layer of oil
on top of the yeast and glucose mixture.

....

....

....

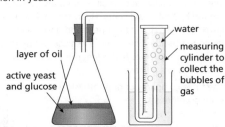

layer of oil

active yeast
and glucose

water

measuring
cylinder to
collect the
bubbles of
gas

b) Explain why it is better to collect the bubbles of gas in a measuring cylinder than count them.

....

....

1 Why are plants important?

Plants as producers

People grow and use plants for many reasons:

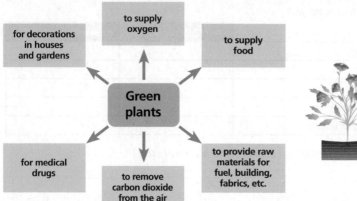

for decorations in houses and gardens

to supply oxygen

to supply food

Green plants

for medical drugs

to remove carbon dioxide from the air

to provide raw materials for fuel, building, fabrics, etc.

Plants are an important source of food for people and other animals as plants can make their own food by photosynthesis. Plants are called **producers**. No animal can make their own food; they need to take it in ready-made.

Photosynthesis by green plants also supplies oxygen that animals need for respiration. It also removes carbon dioxide from the air that is made by respiration.

> It is very important that the balance of oxygen and carbon dioxide in the air is maintained. Removing large areas of forests can disturb this balance.

Chemosynthesis

Scientists once thought that photosynthesis in green plants was the only process that produces food. They now know that certain bacteria can use the energy from chemical reactions to make food. This process is called **chemosynthesis**.

These bacteria live in the soil or deep underwater around hydrothermal vents. Hydrothermal vents are cracks in rocks that let out heat and gases such as hydrogen sulfide. The bacteria can use the hydrogen sulfide as a source of hydrogen, rather than using water to make glucose.

The table compares photosynthesis with chemosynthesis:

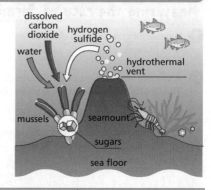

	Photosynthesis	Chemosynthesis
Source of energy	sunlight	chemical reactions
Source of hydrogen atoms	water (H_2O)	hydrogen sulfide (H_2S)
Products	glucose and oxygen	glucose and sulfur

Why are plants important?

Plants as producers

1 Humans use plants to provide raw materials for building.

Name one material from plants that is used for building.

....

2 Write down **three** other uses of plants to humans.

....

....

....

3 Why are plants called producers?

....

4 Explain why cutting down large areas of forests can affect the atmosphere.

....

....

....

Chemosynthesis

5 Where does the energy for chemosynthesis come from?

....

6 Name **two** places where chemosynthetic bacteria live.

....

7 State whether each of the following statements about photosynthesis and chemosynthesis is **true** or **false**.

a) Photosynthesis needs light but chemosynthesis does not. ....

b) Photosynthsis makes glucose. ....

c) Chemosynthesis makes glucose. ....

d) Photosynthesis and chemosynthesis both make oxygen. ....

e) Photosynthesis uses hydrogen sulfide. ....

f) Chemosynthesis uses hydrogen sulfide. ....

1 What is photosynthesis?

Exploring photosynthesis

Scientists now know that this is the equation for photosynthesis:

carbon dioxide $+$ water $\xrightarrow{\text{light energy}}$ glucose $+$ oxygen

This equation was discovered in several steps:
- A scientist called Van Helmont experimented growing a willow tree in a container. He found that plant growth was not only due to minerals from the soil. Plants need other substances.
- Joseph Priestley showed that plants produce oxygen.
- Modern experiments using radioactive carbon dioxide and water have shown that both carbon dioxide and water are needed for photosynthesis.

Where does photosynthesis happen?

The light energy for photosynthesis is trapped by a green chemical called **chlorophyll**. This is found in plant cells in structures called **chloroplasts**.

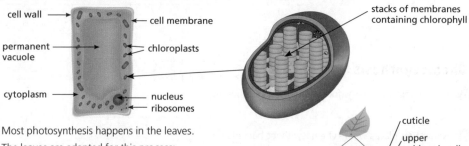

cell wall
cell membrane
permanent vacuole
chloroplasts
cytoplasm
nucleus
ribosomes

stacks of membranes containing chlorophyll

Most photosynthesis happens in the leaves.

The leaves are adapted for this process:
- leaves are thin so that light and gases can penetrate them
- most of the chloroplasts are in the **palisade cells** close to the top of the leaf to get most sunlight
- the **spongy cells** have air spaces so carbon dioxide can diffuse into the leaf
- there are **pores (stomata)** in the **lower epidermis** to let in carbon dioxide.

cuticle
upper epidermis cells
chloroplasts
palisade cells
spongy cells
lower epidermis cells
pore

What substances are made from glucose?

Plants do not feed so they need to make everything they need to survive from glucose made by photosynthesis. The glucose is sent around the plant and converted into different substances:

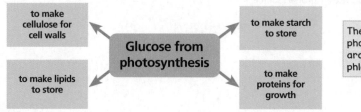

to make cellulose for cell walls

to make starch to store

Glucose from photosynthesis

to make lipids to store

to make proteins for growth

The sugar made in photosynthesis is sent around the plant in the phloem sieve tubes.

What is photosynthesis?

Exploring photosynthesis

1 Name the **two** chemicals that are needed for photosynthesis.

....

2 The diagram shows one of Joseph Priestley's experiments.

| Closed jar: plant did not survive | Closed jar: animal did not survive | Closed jar: animal and plant did survive |

Explain why both the animal and plant survived when they were in the closed jar together.

....

....

Where does photosynthesis happen?

3 Complete the sentences using words from this list.

| cell wall | cytoplasm | chloroplasts | nucleus | vacuole |

Photosynthesis takes place in small structures called ....

These structures are found in the .... of the cell.

4 Look at the diagram of a section through a leaf.

Which letter labels each of these structures?

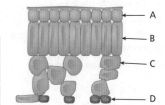

a) The cells where most photosynthesis happens ☐

b) The cells that have air spaces between them ☐

c) The structure that lets gases in and out of the leaf ☐

What substances are made from glucose?

5 Why do plants convert some of their glucose to cellulose?

....

6 What do plants use proteins for?

....

1 How can we investigate photosynthesis?

Investigating stomata

We have already seen that leaves have tiny pores on their lower surface called **stomata**. (One pore is called a stoma.) The stomata allow carbon dioxide into the leaf for **photosynthesis**.

The problem plants have is that they can lose too much water through the stomata. Therefore, stomata close at night to reduce water loss.

> The size of the stoma is controlled by two cells called **guard cells**. When they swell up, the stoma opens. When they shrink, the stoma closes.

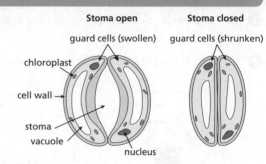

It is possible to count the number of stomata on a leaf using a light microscope.

This is the method:
- Paint the lower surfaces of a leaf with a thin layer of clear nail varnish.
- When it is dry, peel off the nail varnish using forceps.
- Put the piece of dried nail varnish on a microscope slide.
- Add a drop of water and a cover slip.
- Look at it under a microscope.

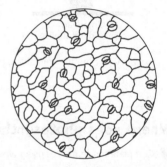

Measuring the rate of photosynthesis

Different plants photosynthesise at different rates. The rate of photosynthesis of a single plant will also be affected by:
- temperature
- concentration of carbon dioxide available
- how bright the light is.

It is easiest to measure the rate of photosynthesis using pondweed. This is because you can count the number of bubbles of oxygen given off in one minute. The more bubbles, the faster the rate of photosynthesis.

This is the apparatus used:

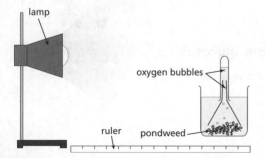

To investigate the effect of temperature, the experiment can be repeated with the water in the beaker at different temperatures.

The distance between the lamp and the pondweed should be kept constant.

> If the effect of temperature is investigated, then the temperature is called the **independent variable**. The rate of photosynthesis (number of bubbles) is called the **dependent variable**.

1) How can we investigate photosynthesis?

Investigating stomata

1 a) When do plants close their stomata?

....

b) Explain why plants do not need their stomata open at that time.

....

....

2 What happens to guard cells to make stomata close?

....

3 The diagram on page 22 shows the image of stomata made using nail varnish.

The area seen under the microscope is 0.1mm².

Calculate how many stomata would be in 1mm² of the leaf's surface.

....

....

Measuring the rate of photosynthesis

4 The rate of photosynthesis is affected by temperature.

Write **two** other factors that could affect the rate of photosynthesis.

....

5 How can you measure the rate of photoynthesis in pondweed?

....

....

6 A student investigated the effect of temperature on the rate of photosynthesis in pondweed. The graph shows their results.

a) What is the independent variable in this experiment?

....

b) At what temperature was the rate of photosynthesis fastest?

....

c) Explain why it is important to keep the distance between the lamp and the pondweed constant during this experiment.

....

....

....

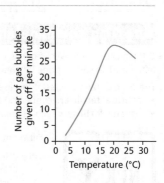

1 Why do plants need minerals?

Absorbing and moving minerals

When the stomata in leaves are open, water vapour diffuses out of the leaf.

This water loss is called **transpiration**.

This causes water to be pulled up the xylem vessels from the roots.

The xylem vessels are specially adapted for transporting water:
- their cells have no end walls so they form one continuous tube
- their walls are strengthened by a substance called **lignin**, which stops the vessels collapsing.

> Water and minerals only move in one direction in xylem vessels - upwards from the roots to the leaves.

In the roots, water is absorbed from the soil by many tiny **root hairs**.

Minerals are dissolved in the water and so are transported up to the leaves in the xylem vessels.

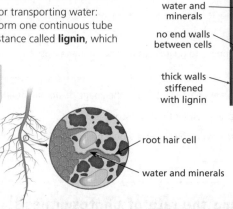

one way only

water and minerals

no end walls between cells

thick walls stiffened with lignin

root hair cell

water and minerals

What do plants use minerals for?

Plants can make sugars using photosynthesis. These sugars contain carbon, hydrogen and oxygen. However, to make certain other substances they need other elements. These elements are supplied by minerals.

Element needed	Mineral supply	Use in the plant	Symptoms caused by lack of the mineral
nitrogen	nitrates	making proteins	stunted growth
magnesium	magnesium ions	making chlorophyll	yellow leaves
phosphorus	phosphates	making DNA	poor root growth

Boosting the minerals in soil

Growing crops removes minerals from the soil. Farmers therefore need to find ways to replace these minerals. This can be done by adding **fertilisers**.

There are different types of fertilisers that farmers can use:
- **artificial fertilisers** containing the minerals plants need
- **organic fertilisers** such as animal manure or compost.

> Organic fertilisers will need to be decomposed in the soil to release the minerals.

Different fertilisers contain different proportions of minerals.

They often have NPK figures on the label. (N = nitrogen, P = phosphorus and K = potassium.) The figures give the proportions of each of these minerals in the fertiliser.

> Different crops need different amounts of each mineral so farmers can choose the fertiliser to suit their crop.

Why do plants need minerals?

Absorbing and moving minerals

1 Write down the scientific name for the diffusion of water out of leaves.

2 Complete these sentences using words from this list.

| any | lignin | one | phloem | pulled | pushed | starch | stomata | xylem |

When water is lost from leaves it causes water in the .... vessels to be

.... up from the roots. The vessels are strengthed by a substance called

.... The water in the vessels can move in .... direction.

3 Explain the function of root hairs.

What do plants use minerals for?

4 Name the elements found in sugars.

5 Why do plant leaves look yellow if grown in a soil that is low in magnesium?

6 Explain why plants need to take in nitrates to make proteins.

Boosting the minerals in soil

7 A farmer uses this artificial fertiliser on some crops.

a) What does the letter K stand for on the bag of fertiliser?

b) The fertiliser in the bag contains 30kg of nitrogen.
Calculate the mass of phosphorus in the bag.

c) Explain why the artificial fertiliser in the bag will act more quickly on the crops than adding manure to the fields.

(1) What is a food web?

What are the feeding relationships?

A **food chain** describes what organisms feed on in a habitat. This is an example of a food chain:

grass → rabbit → fox

The **trophic level** describes the position of an organism in a food chain:
- **producers**, like the grass, are at the start of a food chain and make the food from photosynthesis (or chemosynthesis)
- **primary consumers**, like the rabbit, eat the producers
- **secondary consumers**, like the fox, eat the primary consumers.

Organisms are also classified depending on the type of food they eat rather than their position in a food chain:
- primary consumers are **herbivores** because they eat plant material
- all other consumers are **carnivores** because they eat animals
- if the consumers kill animals and eat them, they are called **predators**
- the animal that is killed by a predator is called **prey**.

However, in nature it is rare for one organism just to eat one type of food. This means that a food chain often becomes a **food web**, which shows all the possible feeding relationships.

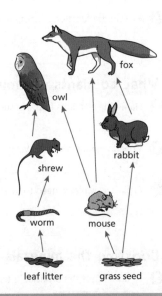

An organism might be at a different trophic level depending on what it is eating. If the owl in this food web eats a mouse, it is a secondary consumer but if it eats a shrew, it is a **tertiary consumer**.

How is energy transferred?

The arrows in a food chain show what organisms eat, but they also show the flow of energy.
- The energy enters a food chain usually from the sun.
- It is then converted to chemical energy in substances such as sugars and proteins.
- These substances are passed along the food chain as one organism eats another.

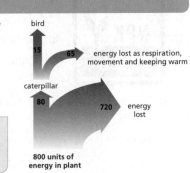

bird
15   65   energy lost as respiration, movement and keeping warm
caterpillar
80   720   energy lost
800 units of energy in plant

As energy is transferred through a food chain, it is lost from the food chain at each stage through processes such as respiration. This means less and less energy is left for each consumer.

1) What is a food web?

What are the feeding relationships?

1 Complete these sentences by writing words in the gaps.

a) The position of an organism in a food chain is called its ....

b) The organisms at the start of a food chain are called ....

c) Animals in the next level of the food chain are called ....

These animals are herbivores because they only eat .... material.

d) Secondary consumers are all carnivores because thay eat ....

2 The diagram shows a food web from the sea.

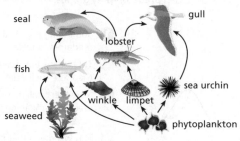

a) Name the **two** producers in this food web.

....

b) What organisms do gulls eat?

....

c) How many organisms are primary consumers in this food web?

....

d) Seals are described as predators. Explain why.

....

e) How many organisms are carnivores in this food chain?

....

How is energy transferred?

3 Write down **one** way that energy is lost from a food chain.

....

4 Food chains do not usually have more than about five trophic levels.

Suggest a reason why.

....

....

1) What is interdependence?

Looking at predator-prey graphs

All organisms rely on other organisms for certain resources. This is called **interdependence**.

Feeding relationships are the most common types of interdependence.

The numbers of predators and their prey are usually constant in a habitat. They are said to be in **equilibrium**. However, sometimes there is a change in the habitat and this might affect the equilibrium. This change could be:

- unusual weather conditions, such as a very cold winter
- a disease that kills the predator, the prey or the prey's food
- release of poisonous chemicals by humans.

Scientists can study the effect of changes in the habitat by plotting graphs to show how the numbers of predators and prey change. These are called **predator–prey graphs**.

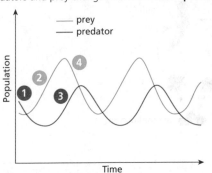

1 Something might cause the number of predators to fall.

2 This means that fewer prey will be eaten so therefore their numbers increase.

3 Now there will be more food for the predators, meaning their numbers will increase.

4 This will mean that more prey will be eaten, causing their numbers to fall, and so on.

Human effects on food chains

One way that humans can affect organisms in a food chain is by releasing poisonous chemicals. These are called **toxins**.

There are different ways that toxins can enter food chains:

- fertilisers dissolve in water and are washed off the fields by rain into rivers and reservoirs
- pesticides used by farmers to kill weeds or insects can be taken in by small organisms
- chemicals released from factories or power stations can fall from the air or pass into rivers.

Sometimes a toxin stays in a prey organism and is not broken down.

This means that the toxin will build up in predators, as they will eat more and more prey. This is called **bioaccumulation**.

Often it is only the top consumer that is killed by the toxin as it has the highest concentration in its body.

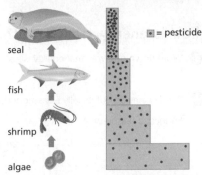

= pesticide

seal

fish

shrimp

algae

number of organisms

1 What is interdependence?

Looking at predator–prey graphs

1 Draw lines to match each biological term with its definition.

Interdependence	A chart showing how the numbers of predators and prey change
Equilibrium	When the numbers of predators and prey are constant
Predator–prey graph	When two organisms rely on each other for resources

2 The graph shows how the numbers of hares and lynx changed in a habitat.

Key

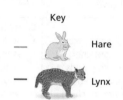

— Hare

— Lynx

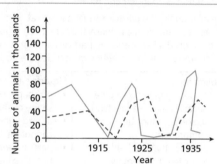

a) Which animal is the predator in this relationship?

....

b) Explain how and why the numbers of hares varied during the years shown on the graph.

....

....

....

Human effects on food chains

3 What are toxins?

....

4 How can pesticides end up in food chains?

....

....

....

5 Explain how bioaccumulation of pesticides can occur in food chains.

....

....

....

② What is the particle model?

Scientific models

Scientists use **models** (which may be diagrams, 3D models or animations) to explain observations and ideas. Good models can also be used to make **predictions** if variables change. Models are useful to help visualise something we cannot see.

As models are a simplified version of what is really happening, they all have limitations. Often, more than one model is used to represent the same thing. So, it is important to evaluate each model and choose the best one to use in each situation.

States of matter

Anything that takes up space and mass is called **matter**. The **particle model** can be used to represent how matter is arranged and moves in each state of matter.

Like all models, the particle model has limitations:
* particles are identical unless they are given different colours
* the individual atoms in the particles are not shown
* intermolecular forces between particles are not shown.

> A substance in the gas state is the least dense and has the most energy compared to the same substance in a solid state.

Solids have:	Liquids have:	Gases have:
• a fixed shape and volume • particles that are touching, so solids cannot be compressed • particles that are held in an ordered pattern by very strong, attractive intermolecular forces • particles that vibrate around a fixed position, so solids cannot be poured.	• no shape, so liquids take the shape of their container • a fixed volume, so liquids cannot be compressed • particles that are touching but the intermolecular forces are not as strong as in a solid so there is no pattern • particles that are moving past each other and so a liquid can be poured.	• no fixed shape or volume as there are only very weak intermolecular forces and they will diffuse to fill the container • particles that are widely spaced and rarely touch, so gases can be compressed • particles that move randomly in all directions and so gases can be poured.

Using the particle model

The particle model can be used to explain changes like **distillation**.

The two substances in the diagram are shown as two different coloured particles and the arrangement of the particles suggests what state they are in.

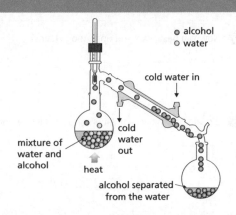

alcohol
water
cold water in
cold water out
mixture of water and alcohol
heat
alcohol separated from the water

② What is the particle model?

Scientific models

1 State whether each of the following statements is **true** or **false** by putting a tick in the correct column.

		True	False
a)	Models are a type of observation		
b)	All models can be used to make predictions		
c)	All models will have limitations		
d)	The same observation may need more than one model to explain it		
e)	Models can be useful to help visualise something we cannot see		

States of matter

2 **a)** Explain why solids like ice cubes cannot be poured. Use ideas about forces between particles in your answer.

....

b) Draw a particle diagram to show the arrangement of particles in a glass of drinking water.

```



```

c) Describe the movement of the particles in a gas.

....

Using the particle model

3 Look at the particle model diagram of distillation on the opposite page. Draw lines to match the part of the diagram on the left to the correct explanation on the right.

Liquid mixture	One colour of particle, particles are still touching but not a regular arrangement

Gaseous alcohol	More than one colour of particle, particles are still touching but not a regular arrangement

Liquid alcohol	One colour of particle, particles not touching and in a random arrangement

② What is changing state?

Changing state

When a substance changes state, only the movement and position of the particles change. This means that changing state is a **physical change**. Substances can change state if you add or remove **heat (thermal energy)**.

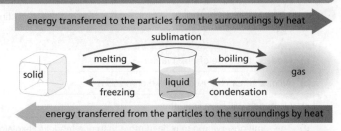

energy transferred to the particles from the surroundings by heat

sublimation

solid — melting → liquid — boiling → gas

freezing ← ← condensation

energy transferred from the particles to the surroundings by heat

Melting point and boiling point

The graph shows the heating of an ice cube:
- The temperature increases as you heat the ice until the melting point is reached at 0°C.
- The melting point is where a pure substance changes state from a solid to a liquid. At this point, the temperature does not change as all the heat (thermal energy) is being used to overcome the strong intermolecular forces between water particles in the ice.
- Once the ice has melted, the temperature will rise again until the boiling point is reached at 100°C.
- The boiling point is where a pure substance changes state from a liquid to a gas. At this point, the temperature does not change as all the energy is being used to pull the water particles apart to form steam.

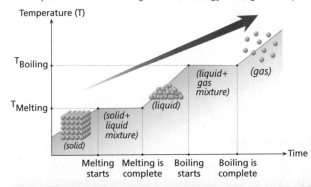

Temperature (T)

$T_{Boiling}$

$T_{Melting}$

(solid)

(solid+ liquid mixture)

(liquid)

(liquid+ gas mixture)

(gas)

Melting starts | Melting is complete | Boiling starts | Boiling is complete

Time

The melting and boiling point of an unknown substance can be used to identify it, by being measured and compared to databases to find out the name of the substance.

Latent heat is the energy that is added to a substance as it changes state. This is the energy needed to overcome the intermolecular forces.

Evaporation and boiling

Both **evaporation** and boiling involve changing a liquid into a gas and are physical changes. However, there are some key differences:

Evaporation	Boiling
• Happens at any temperature between the melting point and boiling point of the substance • A slow process • Only happens at the surface • Energy comes mainly from kinetic energy of the substance	• Only happens at boiling point • Whole liquid changes to a gas • Energy comes mainly from the substance's surroundings

2 What is changing state?

Changing state

1 Complete the table below to name the changes of state that are being described. The first one has been done for you.

Name	State at the start	State at the end
melting	solid	liquid
a)	solid	gas
b)	liquid	gas
c)	gas	liquid
d)	liquid	solid

Melting point and boiling point

2 a) What is the melting point of water? ....

b) What is the boiling point of water? ....

3 Explain why the melting point is always lower than the boiling point for any pure substance.

....

....

....

4 Draw lines to match each key term with its definition.

Melting point		The energy used to overcome intermolecular forces to change state
Boiling point		The temperature at which a pure substance changes from being a solid to a liquid
Latent heat		The temperature at which a pure substance changes from being a liquid to a gas

Evaporation and boiling

5 Decide which of the following statements about evaporation and boiling are true by ticking the correct options.

a) Evaporation and boiling are both physical changes. ☐

b) Boiling can happen at any temperature. ☐

c) Evaporation only happens at the surface of the liquid. ☐

d) Evaporation uses energy mainly from the surroundings. ☐

How can the particle model be used to explain properties?

Brownian motion and viscosity

Both liquids and gases are fluids as their particles move randomly in all directions and can move past each other. The random movement of particles in a fluid is called **Brownian motion**. As the particles are too small to see, we cannot observe Brownian motion directly, but we can see the effects. Solid particles move randomly as they are hit by the fluid particles.

Viscosity is the word used to describe how easy it is for a substance to be poured and to flow. Fluids with a low viscosity can be easily poured because the particles can easily slide over each other due to weak intermolecular forces of attraction.

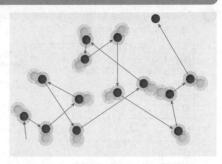

Pressure, expansion and compression

Pressure is caused by moving particles hitting the sides of the container. If there are more collisions with the side of the container, the pressure will increase. Pressure can be increased by:
- decreasing the volume   • heating   • adding more particles.

All particles take up space and have volume. When a substance is heated, the particles gain more kinetic energy and move around more. The particles themselves do not change size or shape but, because they are moving more, the material takes more space. So, substances **expand** and take up more space when heated.

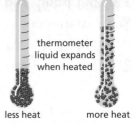

thermometer liquid expands when heated

less heat   more heat

Each state of matter has a different amount of space between the particles. When a substance is **compressed**, the particles are pushed closer together and the substance takes up less volume. But, the particles themselves do not change shape or volume.

> Gases can be compressed a lot as there is a large amount of space between the particles. If a gas is put under extremely high pressure, the particles become so close that the gas changes state into a liquid.

Understanding pressure (air plunger experiment)

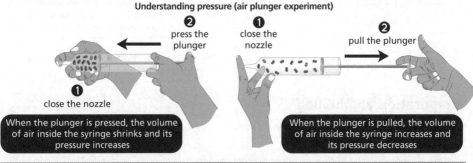

2 press the plunger   **1** close the nozzle   **2** pull the plunger

1 close the nozzle

When the plunger is pressed, the volume of air inside the syringe shrinks and its pressure increases

When the plunger is pulled, the volume of air inside the syringe increases and its pressure decreases

Dissolving

A substance will **dissolve** if the intermolecular forces between the particles of a substance are less than the intermolecular forces between the substance and the solvent. As temperature increases, the solubility of liquids and gases decreases.

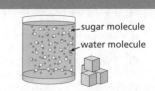

sugar molecule
water molecule

How can the particle model be used to explain properties?

Brownian motion and viscosity

1 **a)** What is Brownian motion?

....

b) Which states of matter have Brownian motion?

....

2 Explain why cooking oil is less viscous than honey at room temperature. Use the idea of forces between particles in your answer.

....

....

....

....

....

Pressure, expansion and compression

3 List **three** ways to increase the gas pressure in a balloon.

....

....

4 Decide if the following statements are about expansion, compression or both. Put a tick in the correct column(s) to show your answer.

	Expansion	Compression
a) Substance takes up more volume		
b) Substance takes up less volume		
c) More space between the particles		
d) Less space between the particles		

Dissolving

5 How does the temperature affect the solubility of gases?

....

6 Explain why gas particles dissolve into a solvent.

....

....

....

....

2 What is density?

Density

Density is a measure of how heavy something is for its size (volume). In dense materials:
- the particles are close together
- there is very little space between the particles.

Usually, for the same material:
- a gas is less dense than a liquid
- a liquid is less dense than a solid.

Density and states of matter

gas   liquid   solid

low density   high density

> Water is an exception to the rule. Liquid water is more dense than solid water (ice). This is why ice floats on water.

To calculate density, you need to:
- measure mass – use a top pan balance to get a value of the mass of a substance
- measure volume:

  – for a regular cuboid shape you can calculate the volume by: volume of cuboid (cm³) = length (cm) × width (cm) × height (cm)
  – for an irregular shape you need to measure the volume by displacement of water using a Eureka can and a measuring cylinder to measure the volume of the displaced water.

> 3D shapes that are not prisms, cuboids, cones or spheres are described as irregular shapes.

Once you have the values for mass and volume you can use the following equation to calculate density:

density (g/cm³) = mass (g) ÷ volume (cm³)

Floating and sinking

A less dense material will float on top of a more dense material. For example:

Cooking oil and water are immiscible liquids and form layers. As cooking oil has a density of 0.93 g/cm³ and water has a density of 1.00 g/cm³, the oil always floats on the water.

Sand is insoluble in water, but sand has a density of 1.5 g/cm³ and so water will float on sand.

When substances are heated, they expand and their density decreases. So, as air gets heated, the spaces between the gas particles increase and the air expands. This means there are the same number of particles, but they take up a greater volume and so density decreases. The warm air will rise and this is how a hot air balloon rises.

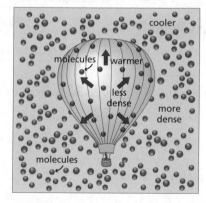

cooler

molecules   warmer

less dense

more dense

molecules

2 What is density?

Density

1 Which state of matter has the lowest density?

2 What measuring instrument is used to measure mass?

3 What unit is volume measured in?

4 **a)** Give the equation to calculate density.

b) Calculate the density of a 10 cm³ block of aluminium with a mass of 27g. Give the units for your answer.

Floating and sinking

5 Table 1 shows the density of different substances.

Substance	Density (g/cm³)
Water	1
Syrup	1.3
Cooking oil	0.93
Polystyrene foam	1.06

In each of the pairs of materials given below, decide which material would float and which material would sink.

a) Water and cooking oil   Floats: _____ Sinks: _____
b) Water and syrup   Floats: _____ Sinks: _____
c) Cooking oil and syrup   Floats: _____ Sinks: _____
d) Water and polystyrene foam   Floats: _____ Sinks: _____
e) Cooking oil and polystyrene foam   Floats: _____ Sinks: _____
f) Syrup and polystyrene foam   Floats: _____ Sinks: _____

② What is concentration?

Solutions

Solutions are transparent mixtures made from one substance dissolving and fitting into the gaps between the liquid particles of another substance.

> Solutions are made because the intermolecular forces of attraction between the solution and the solvent are stronger than the solute alone.

When a solution is made:
- the mass of the solution = mass of the solvent + mass of solute
- the volume of the solution is usually the same as the volume of the solvent.

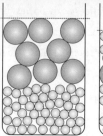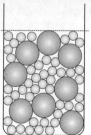

Mass is always conserved. But sometimes the volume of the solution will be less than the volume of the solvent: When alcohol (green) and water (blue) mix, there are very strong intermolecular forces of attraction between them, which results in smaller gaps between the particles than in each pure substance. So, the volume is less than the combined volume of each liquid.

Concentration and dilution

Concentration is a measure of how much substance there is in an amount of space. So, for a solution it is a measure of the mass of solute in the volume of solution. Concentration of a solution can be calculated by:

concentration (g/cm³) = mass of solute (g) ÷ volume of solvent (cm³)

When a solution is made between two liquids, then concentration is usually measured in 'volume per cent' with the unit %. This can be calculated by:

concentration = (volume of solute ÷ volume of solution) × 100%

When water is added to a solution, the concentration of the solution is reduced and the solution becomes more dilute.

A, B and C are all solutions and have the same volume. A is the most concentrated as it has the most solute (green) particles and B is the most dilute with the fewest solute particles.

water molecule   solute molecule

A 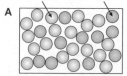   B 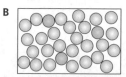   C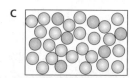

Pressure

The concentration of a gas is the same as the pressure of the gas. So, when the concentration of the gas increases, there are more gas particles in the same space and more collisions with the container, leading to higher pressure.

low pressure 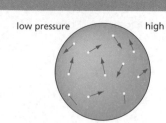   high pressure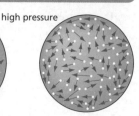

② What is concentration?

Solutions

1 Decide whether each of the following statements is **true** or **false** by putting a tick in the correct column.

	True	False
a) Solutions are always transparent		
b) The mass of the solution is the same as the mass of the solvent		
c) The volume of the solution is the same as the volume of the solvent + the volume of solute		
d) Solvents dissolve into solutes		

2 A student makes a salt solution where 1.2 g of salt is dissolved in 230 g of water.

What is the mass of the solution?

3 A student makes a 25 g sugar solution with 0.5 g of sugar.

What is the mass of the solvent?

Concentration and dilution

4 A student makes a salt solution where 0.5 g of salt is dissolved in 200 cm³ of water.

What is the concentration of the solution? Give the units in your answer.

5 A student makes an alcoholic solution where 50 cm³ of ethanol is dissolved into 100 cm³ of water.

What is the concentration of solution? Give the units in your answer.

6 Describe how to dilute a salt solution.

Pressure

7 Explain why increasing the concentration of a gas increases the pressure of the gas.

② What is diffusion?

Diffusion

Diffusion is the movement of a substance from **high concentration** to **low concentration**. It is a passive physical change and does not need any energy to happen.

- Diffusion occurs because the particles move randomly in all directions.
- The particles move down the concentration gradient from areas of high concentration to areas of low concentration.
- Diffusion happens until the mixture is the same throughout and **equilibrium** has been reached.

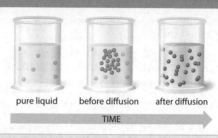

pure liquid   before diffusion   after diffusion

TIME

Diffusion happens until the substances are fully mixed and the concentration is the same throughout the material. This is known as **equilibrium**.

Rate of diffusion

The rate of diffusion is how quickly the substances mix. It can be increased by:
- increasing the temperature – each particle in the substance has more kinetic energy so they move faster
- increasing the concentration gradient.

States of matter and diffusion

Temperature can be measured in degrees celsius, degrees fahrenheit, or using the Kelvin scale.

At absolute zero (-273°C or 0K) all substances are:
- solids
- have no moving particles
- have no kinetic energy.

So, at absolute zero, diffusion cannot happen.

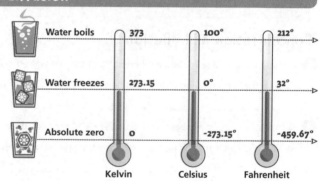

Water boils	373	100°	212°
Water freezes	273.15	0°	32°
Absolute zero	0	-273.15°	-459.67°
	Kelvin	Celsius	Fahrenheit

Diffusion is very slow in solids as the particles are just vibrating and do not move. However, as particles move randomly in all fluids, diffusion happens easily.

The diagram shows diffusion in a gas. In gases, the particles are spread out more and move faster than in liquids. So, diffusion happens faster in gases than in liquids.

When gases are separated they cannot diffuse. But when they can mix, diffusion always happens until all the gases are throughly mixed.

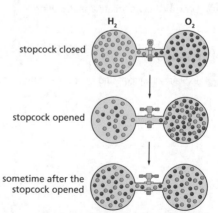

H_2 O_2

stopcock closed

stopcock opened

sometime after the stopcock opened

② What is diffusion?

Diffusion

1 Decide whether each of the following statements is **true** or **false** by putting a tick in the correct column.

	True	False
a) Diffusion needs energy		
b) Diffusion is a physical change		
c) Particles diffuse from high concentration to low concentration		
d) Diffusion happens until equilibrium is reached		
e) Particles moving randomly in all directions causes diffusion		

2 Draw a particle diagram to show a mixture of two substances that have diffused and are at equilibrium.

Rate of diffusion

3 Suggest **two** ways in which the rate of diffusion can be speeded up.

....

....

States of matter and diffusion

4 What temperature is absolute zero on the Celsius scale?

....

5 Which state of matter has the fastest rate of diffusion?

Tick the correct answer.

solid ☐

liquid ☐

gas ☐

② What are the properties of mixtures?

Alloys

An **alloy** is an example of a mixture made mainly of metals. Some examples of alloys include:
- **Steel** – made from iron (Fe) and carbon (C). It is used to make bridges because it rusts more slowly than pure iron.
- **Brass** – made from copper (Cu) and zinc (Zn). Unlike most metals, brass cannot make a spark and so it is used to make containers to mix gunpowder.
- **Bronze** – made from a mixture of copper (Cu) and tin (Sn). Although all metals are sonorous, bronze will continue to make a sound for a long time after being struck so it is used to make bells.

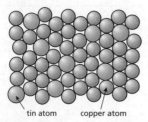

tin atom   copper atom

Mixtures are made when there is more than one substance not chemically joined.

Mixtures can be separated by physical means like filtering, evaporation or distillation.

Properties of alloys

Alloys have all the properties of metals. They are:
- conductors of heat and electricity
- sonorous
- lustrous
- malleable
- ductile.

But alloys also have properties that make them more useful than the pure metals. Alloys are:
- stronger than the pure metals – the different sizes of the atoms makes it more difficult for the layers of atoms to slide over each other
- cheaper than the pure metals as some of the material can be made from cheaper substances.

Pure metal

one type of atom only
regular layers
layers can slide easily
malleable (soft)
Iron

Alloy

mixture of metals
distorted layers
layers cannot slide easily
much harder
Steel

Colloids

A **colloid** is a mixture made with substances in a different state of matter. Examples of colloids include:
- emulsions (e.g. paint, butter) – a mixture of two liquids (one water-based, the other oil-based) that do not normally mix
- foams (e.g. squirty cream) – a mixture of gas bubbles trapped inside a liquid
- gels (e.g. hair gel, jelly) – a mixture of liquid particles floating in a solid
- aerosols (e.g. spray deodorant) – a mixture of particles of liquid or solid dispersed in a gas.

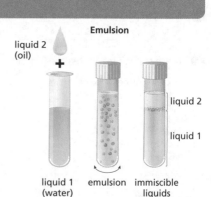

Emulsion

liquid 2 (oil)
+
liquid 2
liquid 1

liquid 1 (water)   emulsion   immiscible liquids

2 What are the properties of mixtures?

Alloys

1 Which elements are found in bronze? Tick the correct answer.

copper and brass ☐

copper and zinc ☐

copper and tin ☐

copper and carbon ☐

2 Explain why alloys are examples of mixtures.

_____

_____

Properties of alloys

3 Give **one** property that alloys have in common with all metals.

_____

4 Why is an alloy of gold used in jewellery rather than pure gold?

_____

5 Explain why steel is harder than pure iron.

_____

_____

Colloids

6 Draw lines to match each example of a colloid on the left to the correct definition on the right.

Foam		A mixture of two liquids (one water-based, the other oil-based) that do not normally mix
Emulsion		A mixture of liquid particles floating in a solid
Aerosol		A mixture of gas bubbles trapped inside a liquid
Gel		A mixture of particles of liquid or solid dispersed in a gas

What are the differences between acids, alkalis, bases and neutral chemicals?

Acids and alkalis

Many foods contain **acids**. This reduces the number of **microbes** growing in the food, which cause it to spoil. Acids:
- contain the element hydrogen
- can dissolve in water
- have a pH < 7
- taste sour – but remember not all acids are safe to taste!

Strong acids like sulfuric acid and hydrochloric acid, or concentrated acids are dangerous and will have a **corrosive hazard warning** on them.

This table lists some of the common acids you would find in a school lab:

Bases react with acids. If a base can dissolve in water, it is called an **alkali**. So, alkalis are a group of bases.

Common acid	Formula	Elements it contains
Hydrochloric	HCl	hydrogen and chlorine
Nitric	HNO_3	hydrogen, nitrogen and oxygen
Sulfuric	H_2SO_4	hydrogen, sulfur and oxygen

Many cleaning products contain alkalis. Alkalis:
- react with acids
- contain the hydroxide particle OH^-
- dissolve in water
- have a pH> 7
- feel soapy – but remember that not all alkalis are safe to touch!

pH is a measure of how acidic a solution is. Water is neither an acid nor an alkali and has a pH = 7, so water is an example of a neutral chemical.

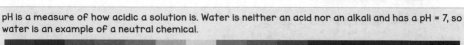

| 0 | 1 | 2 | 3 | 4 | 5 | 6 | 7 | 8 | 9 | 10 | 11 | 12 | 13 | 14 |

Strongly acidic ←————— Weakly acidic → Neutral ← Weakly alkaline —————→ Strongly alkaline

Indicators

Indicators are special chemicals that are a different colour in acid than they are in alkali. They can be solutions that you add to liquid or paper, which is then dipped into the acid or alkali solution. **Litmus** is an example of an indicator that is red in acid, purple in neutral solutions and blue in alkali:

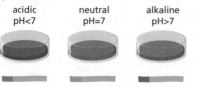

| acidic pH<7 | neutral pH=7 | alkaline pH>7 |

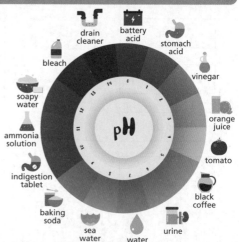

Universal indicator is a mixture of indicators that changes many colours and allows you to measure the pH of a solution.

What are the differences between acids, alkalis, bases and neutral chemicals?

Acids and alkalis

1 Decide if each of the following statements refers to acids, alkalis or neutral chemicals (or more than one). Tick the correct columns to show your answer.

	Acid	Alkali	Neutral chemicals
a) Contain hydroxide			
b) Feel soapy			
c) Taste sour			
d) React with acids			

2 Draw lines to match each pH with the description of the solution.

pH greater than 7		neutral
pH equal to 7		acid
pH less than 7		alkali

3 What does pH measure?

_____

Indicators

4 **a)** What colour would litmus paper be if it was placed in nitric acid?

_____

b) What colour would water turn if litmus solution was added?

_____

5 **a)** What classification would you give a chemical that turned universal indicator red?

_____

b) What colour would you predict cleaning spray would turn universal indicator? Explain why.

_____

_____

② What is neutralisation?

Chemical changes

A chemical change happens when a new substance is made. When we observe a change, observations that a chemical reaction has happened can be seen by:

- bubbling – a new gas is made
- smell – a new gas is made
- colour change – a new substance is made
- the solution becomes cloudy – a new solid has been made.

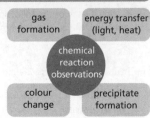

Neutralisation

Neutralisation is a chemical reaction between an **acid** and a **base**. The resulting products are neutral.

Examples of everyday neutralisation include:

- rubbing a dock leaf (weak alkali) on a nettle sting (weak acid) to neutralise it
- taking an anti-acid medicine (weak alkali) to neutralise the excess stomach acid that causes heartburn and indigestion.

> Bee stings are acidic and can be neutralised by bicarbonate of soda, which is a weak alkali. A wasp sting is alkaline and can be neutralised by vinegar, a weak acid.

Neutralisation in the lab

Indicators can be used to monitor a neutralisation reaction in the lab. A technique called **titration** is used to mix acids and alkalis precisely. If universal indicator is used, a whole range of colour changes can be seen.

A burette allows an acid to be added to an alkali gradually. If the acid is added slowly enough, the neutral point (pH 7) can be seen. This point is indicated by the universal indicator in the solution turning green.

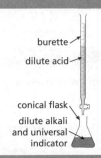

Salts

During neutralisation, the hydrogen atom in the acid gets replaced with a metal atom to make a **salt**. The name of the salt depends on the acid used:

Name of acid	Name in salt	Example of a sodium salt	Use
hydrochloric acid (HCl)	chloride	sodium chloride (NaCl)	To add flavour to food
sulfuric acid (H_2SO_4)	sulfate	sodium sulfate (Na_2SO_4)	To make glass
nitric acid (HNO_3)	nitrate	sodium nitrate ($NaNO_3$)	Added to fertilisers to make plants grow better

② What is neutralisation?

Chemical changes

1 What is a chemical change?

2 A student is carrying out an experiment. He adds vinegar to baking powder and then observes fizzing.

What conclusion can the student draw from this observation?

Neutralisation

3 (Circle) the correct words in the following sentences to explain neutralisation.

Neutralisation is the reaction between an **acid / alkali** and a base. The products of the reaction are **anti-acid / neutral**.

A **bee / wasp** sting is alkaline and can be neutralised by **bicarbonate of soda / vinegar**.

4 How can you neutralise vinegar?

Neutralisation in the lab

5 What substance can you use to monitor a neutralisation reaction in the lab?

Salts

6 Draw lines to match each of the named acids with the type of salt it would make in a neutralisation reaction.

nitric acid		metal chloride

hydrochloric acid		metal sulfate

sulfuric acid		metal nitrate

7 Suggest **one** use for sodium sulfate.

② What happens when acids react?

Metals and acids

- When an acid reacts with a metal, a metal hydroxide and hydrogen gas will be produced.
- The general equation for this reaction is: **metal + acid → metal salt + hydrogen**

Not all metals will react with an acid. Some metals like platinum and gold are described as **inert** because they are so unreactive, and they do not react with acids.

Let's look at an example of a metal reacting with an acid:

Magnesium will react with nitric acid to make magnesium nitrate and hydrogen. Bubbles can be observed as the hydrogen gas is made. The hydrogen gas can be collected and then tested using a lighted splint: a squeaky pop confirms that hydrogen gas is present.

> Often, chemical changes happen in open containers. So when a gas is made, it is lost to the atmosphere and it appears that mass is lost.

Metal carbonates and acids

- When an acid reacts with a metal carbonate, a metal oxide, water and carbon dioxide gas will be produced.
- The general equation for this reaction is: **metal carbonate + acid → metal salt + water + carbon dioxide**

The carbon dioxide gas can be collected or blown through limewater, which turns from colourless to cloudy.

Let's look at a specific example:

calcium carbonate	+	hydrochloric acid	→	calcium chloride	+	carbon dioxide	+	water
$CaCO_3$	+	2HCl	→	$CaCl_2$	+	CO_2	+	H_2O

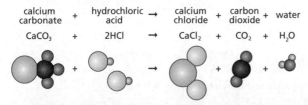

> Calcium carbonate can react with hydrochloric acid to make calcium chloride, water and carbon dioxide.

Metal oxides and acids

- A **neutralisation** reaction happens when an acid reacts with a metal oxide, so a metal salt is produced.
- The general equation for this reaction is: **metal oxide + acid → metal salt + water**

Metal hydroxides and acids

- Metal hydroxides are alkalis and so they can react with acids in a neutralisation reaction.
- The general equation for this reaction is: **metal hydroxide + acid → metal salt + water**

When acids react with an alkali, the hydrogen acid particle combines with the hydroxide alkali particle to make water.

Cl + O(H)(H) Na → (H) O (H) + Na Cl

acid + base → water + salt

Let's look at a specific example:

Hydrochloric acid can react with sodium hydroxide to form water and sodium chloride:

hydrochloric acid + sodium hydroxide → water + sodium chloride

$HCl + NaOH → H_2O + NaCl$

② What happens when acids react?

Metals and acids

1. What is made in a reaction between zinc and hydrochloric acid?

   ....

2. Complete the word equation.

   .... + sulfuric acid → calcium sulfate + ...

3. Describe how you would test a gas to show it was hydrogen.

   ....

   ....

Metal carbonates and acids

4. What is made in a reaction between sodium carbonate and hydrochloric acid?

   ....

5. Complete the word equation.

   .... + ... → calcium chloride + carbon dioxide + water

6. Describe how you would test a gas to show it was carbon dioxide.

   ....

   ....

Metal oxides and acids

7. Which of the following are products of the reaction between magnesium oxide and hydrochloric acid? Tick the correct options.

   oxygen ☐   magnesium carbonate ☐

   magnesium sulfate ☐   hydrogen ☐

   magnesium chloride ☐   water ☐

8. Complete the word equation.

   copper oxide + ... → copper sulfate + ...

Metal hydroxides and acids

9. What is made in a reaction between potassium hydroxide and nitric acid?

   ....

10. Complete the word equation.

    sodium hydroxide + sulfuric acid → .... + ...

② What is combustion?

Combustion

Combustion is the word used in science for burning. Combustion:
- is a chemical change as a new substance is made
- is irreversible
- is **exothermic** as it releases energy to the surroundings
- uses oxygen as a reactant.

To stop a fire, you can:
- remove the fuel, e.g. turn off the gas tap to the Bunsen burner and the flame stops
- prevent oxygen getting to the flame, e.g. smother the flame with a fire blanket
- remove the heat, e.g. use a fire extinguisher to cool the fire.

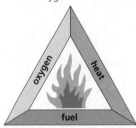

The **fire triangle** is a way of remembering what is needed for a combustion reaction. If one side of the fire triangle is missing, the combustion reaction will stop.

A **fuel** is a store of chemical energy. When it is combusted, it transfers the stored chemical energy to thermal energy store. This thermal energy can heat our homes, cook our food, move our cars and generate electricity.

Hydrocarbons

Hydrocarbons are substances that contain only hydrogen and carbon. Many fuels, such as coal, oil and gas, are examples of hydrocarbons, e.g. butane is a hydrocarbon that is extracted from oil and used as a fuel in camping gas stoves.

Hydrocarbons are combusted when they are used. The type of combustion depends on the amount of oxygen present.

Complete combustion	Incomplete combustion
• Lots of oxygen • Most of the energy is released from the fuel • Clean (blue) flame • General equation: hydrocarbon + oxygen → carbon dioxide + water	• Limited oxygen • Less energy is released from the fuel • Dirty (orange) flame • General equation: hydrocarbon + oxygen → carbon dioxide + water + carbon + carbon monoxide

Products of combustion

When hydrocarbons are combusted, their products can cause harm:
- carbon dioxide is a **greenhouse gas** and causes global climate change
- carbon or soot causes respiratory problems and global dimming
- carbon monoxide is a toxic gas that can poison people and cause death so it is important to get gas appliances regularly serviced to prevent carbon monoxide poisoning.

Acid rain is caused by combusting fuels:
- sulfuric acid is made from the combustion of sulfur impurities in the fuels
- nitric acid is made from car engines where the high temperature and pressure causes nitrogen and oxygen from the air to make acidic gases, which then react with water.

Acid rain can be prevented by:
- removing the sulfur before the fuel is used
- neutralising the fumes from combustion
- using a catalytic converter on the car exhaust pipe.

2 What is combustion?

Combustion

1 Which element is always a reactant in a combustion reaction?

....

2 What is the scientific term used to describe a change that gives out energy?

....

3 Complete the fire triangle to name the things that are needed for a fire.

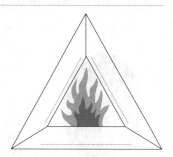

4 How does a fire blanket stop a fire?

....

Hydrocarbons

5 Which **two** elements are in hydrocarbons?

....

6 **a)** Complete the word equation for the complete combustion of propane.

propane + ... → carbon dioxide + ...

b) Complete the word equation for the incomplete combustion of ethane.

oxygen + ... → carbon dioxide + carbon + ... +

....

Products of combustion

7 Draw lines to match each of the products of combustion to its negative consequence.

carbon dioxide	acid rain
carbon (soot)	respiratory problems and global dimming
carbon monoxide	global climate change
oxides of sulfur and nitrogen	toxic gas

What is static charge?

Creating static charge

If you rub a balloon on your hair, it acquires a **static charge**. This charge is made up of tiny particles called **electrons**, which have transferred from atoms in your hair to the balloon.

> Objects that gain electrons are **negatively charged**; objects that lose electrons are **positively charged**.

The effect of static charge can be shown by placing the charged balloon just above small bits of paper on a table. An interaction between electrons on the balloon and charged particles in the paper lifts them up off the table. This interaction is an attractive force that works across the space between the balloon and the table.

> Forces created by static charges are **non-contact forces**.

The space around a charged object is called an **electric field**. If another charged object enters that electric field, an interaction will occur. Imagine one of the charged balloons being surrounded by its own electric field. When the other charged balloon is put into this field, an interaction occurs in the form of a repulsive force.

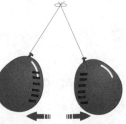

These balloons are both negatively charged as shown by the minus signs. When they are attached by string to the same point on the ceiling, they try to move away from each other.

> Two negatively charged objects repel each other. Two positively charged objects also repel. But a positive object and a negative object attract.

Using static charge

Static charge is used to paint cars:
- The body of a car is given a negative charge and is then surrounded by its own electric field.
- The robotic arms control paint spray guns. The paint emitted is positively charged as it leaves the spray gun.
- The car's electric field pulls the positively charged paint droplets towards it, covering the car evenly. Very little paint ends up on the floor.

Static charge also has other uses:
- Inside factories, electrostatic air cleaners use static charge to remove dust and other pollution from the air.
- Photocopiers use static charge to get a black pigment, called toner, to form the text or image being copied on to paper.

What is static charge?

Creating static charge

1 When you use a plastic comb on your hair, tiny particles called electrons from the atoms in your hair, are transferred to the comb.

If the comb is placed a few centimetres above bits of paper on a table, its static charge attracts some of them.

a) Is the comb charged positive or negative?

....

b) What is the name given to the space surrounding the comb that is affected by its charge?

....

c) Is the force between the charged comb and the bits of paper a non-contact force or a contact force?

....

2 When a glass rod is rubbed with a silk cloth, electrons are transferred from the rod to the cloth.

a) Is the glass rod charged positive or negative?

....

silk cloth

b) Two charged glass rods are moved towards each other so that their electric fields overlap. Will the interaction create a repulsive force or an attractive force between the rods? Explain your answer.

....

....

Using static charge

3 The diagram on the left shows a normal paint spray gun, which does not use static charge. The diagram on the right is an electrostatic spray paint gun. Both guns are spraying red paint.

normal paint spray gun

electrostatic paint spray gun

a) How is the shape of the jet of paint from the electrostatic gun different to the normal gun?

....

b) The paint droplets from the normal paint gun are not charged. The paint droplets from the electrostatic gun are given a positive charge as they leave the gun. Explain why the paint jets have a different shape.

....

....

....

The Earth's gravity

The space around the Earth, where objects experience its force of gravity, is called the Earth's **gravitational field**.

The Earth's gravitational field exerts a force on an apple in a tree. If the apple's stem breaks, the force of gravity causes it to fall faster and faster from the tree to the ground.

When the apple is on the ground, the Earth is still exerting a downward force of gravity on it. However, the apple does not continue to fall because an upward **contact force** is exerted on the apple by the ground.

- The force of gravity on an object is also known as its **weight**. Weight (W), mass (m), and gravitational field strength g are linked by the equation: **W = mg**
- At the Earth's surface, the value of g is about 10 N/kg. This means that a mass of 1 kg experiences a force of gravity of 10 N.
- The mass of the satellite in the diagram above is 1200 kg. So, its weight on the Earth can be found from: W = mg = 1200 × 10 = 12,000 N.

Earth

gravity

Orbiting satellite experiences an attractive gravitational force towards the Earth. The force of gravity stops it from flying off into outer space.

The Earth's gravitational field strength is defined as the gravitational force on a mass of 1 kg. It is given the symbol g and is measured in units of newton per kilogram (N/kg).

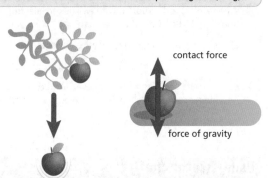

contact force

force of gravity

Space travel

Moving away from the Earth's surface, at the height of the satellite's orbit, the value of g is about 7 N/kg. So, the force of gravity on the 1200 kg satellite in orbit is: W = mg = 1200 × 7 = 8400 N

As you get further away from the Earth's surface, its gravitational field strength decreases.

After escaping from the Earth's gravitational field, a spacecraft is still affected by the Sun's gravitational field.

A spacecraft from Earth heading towards the edge of the Solar System would carry enough fuel to escape from the Earth's gravity. But it will still experience the attractive force of gravity exerted by the Sun.

When the spacecraft runs out of fuel, it uses the gravity of the outer planets to help it on its way.

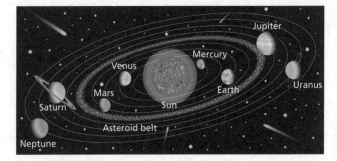

Jupiter

Mercury

Venus

Uranus

Mars

Earth

Saturn

Sun

Asteroid belt

Neptune

How does gravity change in different parts of space?

The Earth's gravity

1 a) What does gravitational field strength mean?

....

b) What is the symbol for gravitational field strength? ....

c) What unit is used for gravitational field strength? ....

2 a) Give the equation that links weight (W), mass (m), and gravitational field strength (g).

....

b) What is the weight of a person of mass 80 kg at the Earth's surface?

The value of g at the Earth's surface is 10 N/kg.

Show your working. .... N

Space travel

3 How does the Earth's gravitational field strength change as you get further away from the Earth's surface?

....

4 NASA's Perseverance Rover landed on Mars in 2021. Its mass is 1000 kg. Calculate the force of gravity exerted by Mars on the Rover.

Gravitational field strength on Mars is 3.7 N/kg.

Show your working. ....

5 A spacecraft (shown not to scale) is on its journey from the Earth to the Moon.

a) How does the force of gravity exerted by the Earth on the spacecraft change as it gets further away from the Earth?

....

b) How does the force of gravity exerted by the Moon on the spacecraft change as it gets closer to the Moon?

....

c) At the positions shown in the diagram, the forces exerted on the spacecraft by the Earth and the Moon are the same size. Add two force arrows to the diagram to show the forces exerted on the spacecraft by the Earth and Moon.

d) Which Solar System object is exerting gravitational forces on the Earth, the Moon, and the spacecraft?

....

Contact force, area and pressure

The picture shows a man walking through the snow. He is wearing boots and is sinking deep into the snow. If he wore skis or used a snowboard, this would significantly increase his area in contact with the ground, which would keep him on, or very close to, the snow's surface.

The **contact force** he exerts on the ground and his contact area on the ground, determines how far he sinks into the snow.

The man's weight is 600N, so he exerts a contact force on the ground of 600N.

To determine his contact area, we can look at his footprints in the snow and estimate the length and width of an imaginary rectangle that roughly covers one footprint:

- Length of the rectangle is measured as 0.25m
- Width of the rectangle is measured as 0.10m
- Area of the rectangle = 0.25 × 0.10
  = 0.025 square metres
- Total contact area (for two shoes) = 0.025 + 0.025 = 0.05 square metres = 0.05 m²

> area = length x width

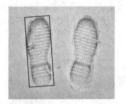

0.10m

0.25m

To consider the effect of both contact force and contact area, we use another quantity called **pressure**.

- Contact force = 600N and contact area = 0.05 m², and pressure = force ÷ area:
- 600 ÷ 0.05 = 12,000 N/m²

> pressure = force ÷ area
> The units of pressure are newton per square metre, written as N/m²

Comparing pressure

If the man in the picture above had been wearing skis, his area in contact with the ground would have been about 8 times larger. This means the pressure he exerted on the snow would be 8 times smaller.

With the pressure much reduced, the skis only sink very slightly into the snow and he would have been able to move more easily and quickly.

> If a force can be spread over a larger area, the pressure is reduced.

RETRIEVE 3 — What causes pressure on the surface of a solid?

Contact force, area and pressure

1. The diagram shows a heavy box on a table.
   The box has a weight of 200 N.

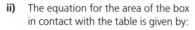

   a) Complete the following sentences:

   i) The contact force exerted on the table by the box has the same value as the

   .... of the box.

   ii) The equation for the area of the box in contact with the table is given by:

   area = width × ....

   b) Determine the values to complete the following statements.

   contact force exerted on table = ... N

   area of box in contact with table = ... m²

   c) Use the equation below to calculate the pressure exerted by the box on the table.

   pressure = force ÷ area

   pressure = ... N/m²

2. A drawing pin is pushed into a notice board with a force of 10 N.
   The area of the point of the pin is 0.0000001 m².

   Calculate the pressure exerted by the drawing pin on the board.

   pressure = ... N/m²

3. An elephant has a weight of 30,000 N. The contact area of each foot on the ground is 0.2 m².

   Calculate the pressure exerted by the elephant when standing on all four feet. Show your working.

   pressure = ... N/m²

Comparing pressure

4. The table shows the weight of, and the pressure exerted on the ground by, three objects.

Object	Weight in newton	Pressure exerted in N/m²
military tank	600,000	100,000
car	18,000	200,000
mountain bike and rider	600	240,000

Explain why the military tank exerts the smallest pressure despite being the heaviest of the three objects.

....

....

3 What causes pressure in a liquid?

How does the particle model represent liquid pressure?

The **particle model** represents a liquid as tiny particles that are very close together. The particles are not arranged in any pattern. There are some gaps, but the particles are mostly touching each other. This is why liquids are very difficult to compress.

- Liquid particles are always moving and bumping into each other.
- They can flow over or alongside each other.
- This means that liquid particles push against the container walls.

liquid particles

> Pressure in a liquid is caused by the liquid particles exerting forces on the container walls. Liquid pressure increases as depth increases.

The liquid pushes against the container walls. The weight of liquid pushes down on the liquid below. Liquids cannot be compressed so at deep levels, the liquid pushes harder on the container walls.

If you put holes in the container shown in the diagram and kept topping up the water, the liquid pressure would create water jets. The bottom jet comes out with the most force.

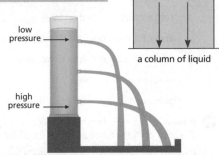

low pressure

high pressure

a column of liquid

Floating and sinking

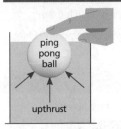

ping pong ball

upthrust

If you try to hold a ping pong ball under water with one finger you will find it is quite difficult. You can feel the water pushing up against the ball. This is called **upthrust**.

The ping pong ball is filled with air, so its weight is very small. As you push down on the ball, the upthrust increases and is larger than the ball's weight, which is why it is so difficult to push the ball under the water.

> The upthrust acting on an object is caused by pressure in the liquid.

Some materials float and some sink. The diagram shows two balls of the same size but made from different materials: wood and steel. Both are solid; there is no air inside them. The matter that makes up the steel ball is packed much more densely than in the wooden ball so the wooden ball is much lighter.

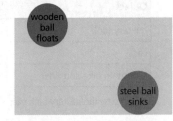

wooden ball floats

steel ball sinks

The balls are placed in a container of water. The upthrust created by the liquid pressure balances the weight of the wooden ball but not the steel ball, which is too heavy.

> A solid object made of a material that is denser than water, will sink in water. But one which is made of material that is less dense than water, floats.

3 What causes pressure in a liquid?

How does the particle model represent liquid pressure?

1 a) Describe the motion of the particles in a liquid.

....

b) Tick the **two** options that best describe the arrangement of particles in a liquid.

large gaps between particles ☐   particles are very close together ☐

particles are arranged in a pattern ☐   particles are not arranged in a pattern ☐

2 As the particles in the beaker move around, they keep pushing against the beaker walls. This causes the liquid to exert pressure.

Explain what causes the pressure at level Y to be greater than at level X.

....

....

....

3 The image shows the wall of a dam. Notice that the wall is much thicker at the bottom than the top.

a) Why is the wall thicker at the bottom?

....

....

b) The red arrow represents the small force exerted by the water near the top of the dam. Add another arrow to represent the size of the force near the bottom of the dam.

water in reservoir →

dam wall

Floating and sinking

4 Blocks of the same size and shape, but different materials, are placed in the beakers containing a liquid, as shown in the diagram.

a) Which beaker contains the block made from the densest material? ☐

b) What is the name given to the force that is balancing the weight of the block in beaker A?

....

c) The beakers contain the same volume of water. Why is the water level in beaker B higher than in beaker A?

....

....

A   B

3) What causes pressure in a gas?

How does the particle model represent gas pressure?

The **particle model** represents a gas as tiny **particles** that move around very quickly and are not arranged in any pattern.

- There are large gaps between the particles, which means there is space to compress gas particles closer together.
- The gas particles collide with each other and with any surface they meet.
- Each time a gas particle collides with a surface it exerts a pushing force.
- Vast numbers of air particles are colliding with your body every second, exerting an overall force of over 100,000 newtons!

gas particles

> **Gas pressure** is the force exerted by gas particles on a surface of area 1 square metre.

Atmospheric pressure

The **atmosphere** is a band of gas surrounding the Earth. The gas, usually referred to as 'air', is mostly made up of nitrogen and oxygen molecules.

> Although air molecules are moving very fast, with average speeds of 500 metres per second, they cannot escape the Earth's gravity.

The gas pressure exerted by the molecules in the atmosphere is called atmospheric pressure. The air closer to the Earth's surface is squashed by the weight of the atmosphere above. So, the air molecules at sea level are pushed closer together than air molecules at high **altitude**, at the top of a mountain, for example.

atmosphere

- Atmospheric pressure at sea level is about 100,000 N/m^2.
- Atmospheric pressure at the summit of Mount Everest is about 30,000 N/m^2.

Every breath you take at the summit contains less than a third of the oxygen molecules your body needs to function normally. This can cause altitude sickness so mountaineers carry oxygen cylinders with them.

> Atmospheric pressure decreases at higher altitudes.

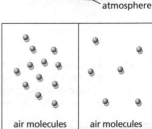

| air molecules at sea level | air molecules at high altitude |

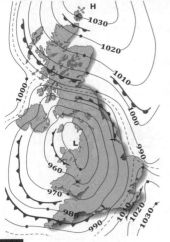

In London, atmospheric pressure typically ranges from 97,000 N/m^2 to 104,000 N/m^2. Atmospheric pressure is measured with a device called a **barometer**.

> Atmospheric pressure at a specific location varies depending on the weather.

The weather map shows a high pressure region, (H), and a low pressure region, (L):

- the blue lines represent a cold front; the blue triangles point in the direction that the cold weather is moving
- the red lines are warm fronts
- the numbers represent atmospheric pressure (e.g. add two zeros to a number on the map (e.g. 1020) to get the pressure 102,000 N/m^2).

3 What causes pressure in a gas?

How does the particle model represent gas pressure?

1 **a)** Describe the motion of the particles in a gas.

....

b) Tick **two** boxes that best describe the arrangement of the particles in a gas.

large gaps between particles ☐   particles are very close together ☐

particles are arranged in a pattern ☐   particles are not arranged in a pattern ☐

2 How do gas particles exert pressure on a surface?

....

Atmospheric pressure

3 What is it that prevents the gas particles in the atmosphere from escaping into outer space?

....

4 What is the difference between the arrangement of air molecules at sea level and at high altitude?

....

5 The graph shows how atmospheric pressure changes with height above sea level.

a) A mountaineer is in the French Alps. Her height above sea level is 2000 m. What is the value of atmospheric pressure at this altitude?

.... N/m²

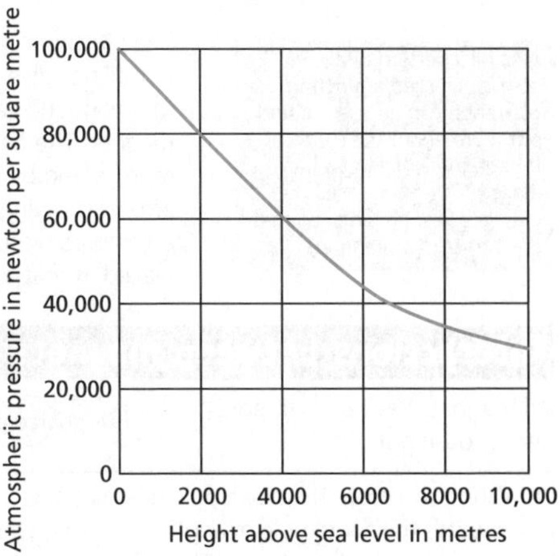

b) The mountaineer continues her climb. On reaching an altitude of 2500 m, she is aware that there is now a risk of altitude sickness. What is the cause of altitude sickness?

....

c) **i)** Continuing her climb, the mountaineer records atmospheric pressure as 60,000 N/m² using a travel barometer. What is the altitude at her location?

.... m

ii) She remains at this location for the night. The following morning, her travel barometer reading has dropped slightly even though her altitude has not changed.

What is the most likely cause of the drop in atmospheric pressure?

....

Graph: Atmospheric pressure in newton per square metre (y-axis, 0 to 100,000) vs Height above sea level in metres (x-axis, 0 to 10,000).

③ What are magnets?

Magnetic fields

A **magnet** is a piece of matter that creates a **magnetic field** in the space that surrounds it. A magnetic field is invisible. Tiny bits of iron can be used to show the magnetic field around a bar magnet; the tiny bits of iron are pushed and pulled by the magnetic field.

> Filings made of iron can be used to show the pattern of a magnetic field because iron is a **magnetic material**.

Other magnetic materials include nickel, steel, cobalt, and neodymium.

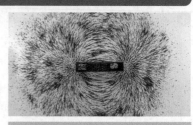

The pattern of curved lines made by the bits of iron shows the shape of the magnetic field.

When a magnetised steel needle is placed on a piece of cork floating in a bowl of water, the needle's magnetic field interacts with the **Earth's magnetic field**. This makes the needle rotate so that one end points towards the Earth's North Pole. This end is called a north seeking pole, or **north pole**. The other end is a **south pole**.

A suspended magnetised needle forms part of a compass. A navigation compass is used by sailors to find their way at sea, and by hikers following maps.

A smaller version of a compass, called a **plotting compass**, can be used to find out more about the shape of the magnetic field of a bar magnet. The red half of the needle gives the direction that the compass is pointing.

The plotting compass and the iron filings give us a picture of the magnetic field of a bar magnet. The field is represented by lines with arrows showing the direction a compass would point when placed at that position.

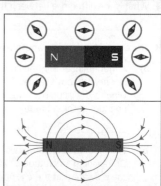

Interactions between magnets

All magnets have a north pole and a south pole.

> Opposite poles of two magnets attract; similar poles repel.

- When you move the north pole of a magnet towards the south pole of another magnet, you can feel an attractive force. This is caused by the interaction of the magnets' fields and is called a **magnetic force**. Since it exists without the magnets touching, it is a **non-contact force**.

attraction

- If you try to push a north pole towards another north pole, or a south pole towards another south pole, the magnetic force is a repulsive non-contact force.

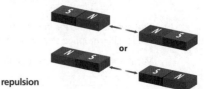

or

repulsion

③ What are magnets?

Magnetic fields

1 Give the name of a magnetic material. ....

2 Describe a situation where a navigation compass is likely to be used.

....

3 A steel nail has been magnetised. A plotting compass is placed near the point of the nail. Which end of the nail – the **head** or the **point** – is a south pole?

....

4 A bar magnet is suspended so it is free to rotate. It rotates, then becomes stationary. To what location on the Earth does the magnet's north pole point?

....

5 This bar magnet has been drawn with some of its magnetic field lines. The two circles represent plotting compasses.

Add arrows to both circles to show the direction that each compass needle would point.

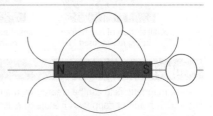

Interactions between magnets

6 Three objects, in turn, are held in the position shown by the dotted rectangle.

State what effect each one has on the north pole of the suspended magnet.

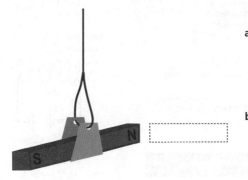

a)

....

b)

....

c) Non-magnetic metal

....

What are the different types of magnet?

Permanent magnets

A **permanent magnet** is a magnet that keeps its magnetic properties. Iron, nickel and cobalt are strongly magnetic materials. They are to be found in most permanent magnets, usually chemically combined, or mixed with other elements.

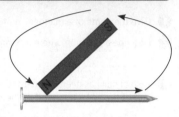

The nail in the diagram is made of steel (iron mixed with carbon). Repeatedly stroking the nail with the north pole of a magnet in the direction shown by the arrows magnetises the nail. The point of the nail becomes a north pole, and the head becomes a south pole.

> A magnetised steel nail will retain its magnetism so long as it is not dropped or hit with a hammer.

Inside the nail, each atom of iron acts like a tiny magnet. The atoms band together in a region within the nail, so their tiny magnets create magnetic fields with the same direction. These regions are called **domains**. The diagram shows a small section of the nail, before and after it has been magnetised.

small section of nail before being magnetised

small section of nail after being magnetised

> Stroking a steel nail with a magnet aligns its domains, giving it permanent magnetism.

Temporary magnets

A weak magnetic field can be created with a piece of wire and a battery. The wire is made of copper with a green plastic coating.

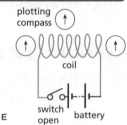

plotting compass

coil

switch open   battery

- When the switch in the circuit is open, no electric current flows and a magnetic field is not created so the plotting compass needles point north.
- When the switch is closed, an electric current is flowing in the coil. The plotting compass needles have changed direction: the coil is now producing a magnetic field. It is an **electromagnet**.

> When an electric current flows in the coil, a magnetic field is created. If the switch is opened, no current flows so the magnetic field disappears.

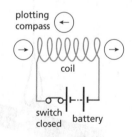

plotting compass

coil

switch closed   battery

A very strong magnetic field, which can be switched on and off as we choose, can be made with a long coil containing a core of soft iron. It is called a **solenoid**.

> An iron cored solenoid, carrying an electric current, creates a strong magnetic field.

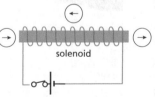

solenoid

This table gives details of the magnets:

Magnet	Type of magnet	Strength of field
bar magnet	permanent	quite strong
electromagnet with air core	temporary	weak
solenoid with iron core	temporary	very strong

What are the different types of magnet?

Permanent magnets

1 Describe what is meant by a permanent magnet.

_____

2 Name **two** elements that are often used in the making of permanent magnets.

_____

3 Complete the sentences **a)** to **c)** using the words in the box.

| domain   magnet   fields   electromagnet   domains |

a) In a magnetic material, each atom acts like a tiny _____.

b) In a magnetic material, a group of atoms band together in a small area called

a _____ where their magnetic _____ are in the same direction.

c) When the material is magnetised, the magnetic fields of all the _____ are all in the same direction.

Temporary magnets

4 What name is given to a magnet created by an electric current?

_____

5 a) What is the name given to a long metal coil?

_____

b) Describe what you would have to do to make a long metal coil create a magnetic field.

_____

c) What change would you make so that the long metal coil created a very strong magnetic field?

_____

d) What would you need to do to make the magnetic field disappear?

_____

6 The table lists some magnets.

For each one, tick the **two** boxes that give its correct description.

Magnet	Permanent	Temporary	Strong field	Weak field
a) bar magnet				
b) electromagnet with air core				
c) solenoid with iron core				

3 How can electromagnets be used?

Advantages of electromagnets

Most useful **electromagnets** consist of a coil, sometimes containing a soft iron core. When a battery is connected to the coil, it drives an electric current around it. This creates the **magnetic field**. Three advantages of an electromagnet compared with a permanent magnet are:

- the magnetic field can be easily switched on or off by connecting or disconnecting the battery
- the size of the electric current can be varied so the strength of the field can be controlled
- the direction of the field can be easily reversed by swapping the battery connections.

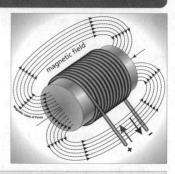

The magnetic field of an electromagnet can be switched on or off, can be made stronger or weaker, and made to change direction.

Useful applications of electromagnets

Some of the uses of electromagnets include:

- loudspeakers
- magnetic locks
- data storage
- headphones
- cranes
- electric bells.

	**Headphones** Each earpiece in a set of headphones contains a permanent magnet and an electromagnet. The interaction between them causes the vibration that produces sound.
	**Crane** A scrap yard crane uses an electromagnet to move iron and steel waste. At the end of the crane is an iron disc containing a coil. When an electric current flows in the coil, the iron disc becomes a strong temporary magnet which attracts the waste. To release the waste at another location, the crane operator switches off the electric current to the coil.
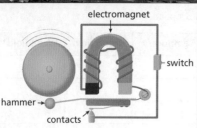	**Electric bell** The electric bell contains a coil wrapped around a U-shaped iron core. Pushing the switch connects the coil to a battery (not shown in the diagram). When the iron core becomes magnetised, it attracts the iron hammer causing it to hit the gong. The process repeats itself producing the ringing sound.

③ How can electromagnets be used?

Advantages of electromagnets

1 **a)** What is an electromagnet made up of?

....

b) What is created when an electric current is supplied to an electromagnet?

....

c) Give **one** advantage of an electromagnet compared with a permanent magnet.

....

Useful applications of electromagnets

2 The two diagrams show the same electromagnetic switching device.
Diagram A shows the device before switch 1 is closed.

a) On diagram A, label the coil of the electromagnet.

b) On diagram A, label the iron core of the electromagnet.

c) Closing switch 1 in diagram A would allow an electric current to flow in the coil. How would this affect the iron core?

....

....

Diagram A

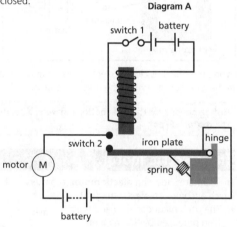

d) Diagram B shows the changes that result from closing switch 1.

Spot **three** ways that diagram B is different from diagram A.

....

....

....

....

Diagram B

e) The changes cause an electric current to be delivered to the motor. If this motor was in a car, it would carry a very large electric current. The device enables the driver to switch on the motor circuit without actually touching it.

Why might this be a good thing?

....

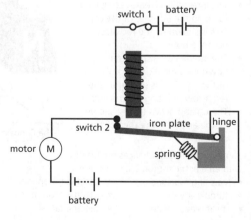

3 What is the motor effect?

Interacting magnetic fields

When two magnets are moved close enough for their magnetic fields to overlap, an interaction occurs. The interaction can be either an **attractive** or **repulsive** force. A similar interaction occurs between a magnet and a magnetic field produced by a wire carrying an electric current:

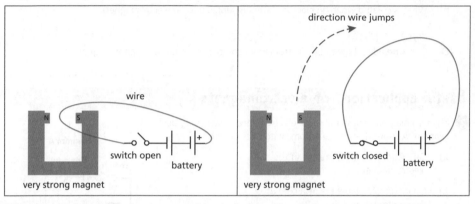

When the switch is closed, electric current flows in the wire. The wire instantly jumps out of the magnet in the direction shown by the dotted red arrow.

Motion caused by the interaction between a permanent magnet and an electromagnet is called the **motor effect**.

The electric motor

The diagram shows an **electic motor**. A battery (not shown in the diagram) is connected to the coil, which becomes an **electromagnet**.

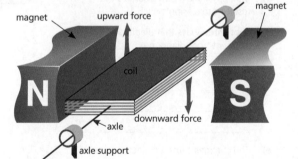

- The coil's magnetic field and the field produced by the magnets interact.
- The interaction creates an upward force on the left side of the coil. This is shown by the red arrow pointing upwards.
- The interaction also creates a downward force on the right side of the coil. This is shown by the red arrow pointing downwards.
- The up and down forces, shown by the arrows make the coil rotate clockwise.

The function of the electric motor is to create rotation.

Some household appliances are fitted with an electric motor. These include:
- washing machine
- tumble dryer
- microwave cooker
- electric tin opener
- electric food mixer
- electric fan.

What is the motor effect?

Interacting magnetic fields

1 **a)** The blue lines in diagram A represent the magnetic field created between north and south poles.

The blue lines in diagram B represent the magnetic field surrounding a wire carrying an electric current delivered by a battery (not shown).

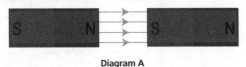

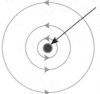

cross secton of a wire carrying an electric current

Diagram A   **Diagram B**

Describe the differences in the patterns of the two magnetic fields.

....

....

b) The wire is disconnected from the battery and placed in between the magnets. When the wire is reconnected to the battery, the two magnetic fields interact, creating the magnetic field shown below. Immediately the wire jumps up out of the field.

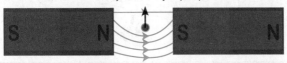

The magnetic force pushes the wire away from the strongest part of the field towards the weakest. Tick the statement that correctly describes a magnetic field.

A magnetic field is strongest where field lines are closer together. ☐

A magnetic field is strongest where field lines are further apart. ☐

The electric motor

2 The diagram shows a simplified electric motor. The coil is represented by a single turn coloured red. When the battery is connected, the coil rotates anticlockwise.

a) Add an arrow to each side of the coil to represent the forces acting on the coil.

b) Suggest a change that would make the coil rotate in the opposite direction.

....

....

c) The commutator is there to help connect the coil to the battery.

Why might it be difficult to connect the coil to the battery?

....

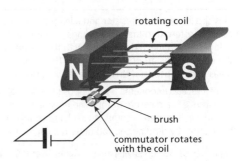

rotating coil

brush

commutator rotates with the coil

③ What is an electric circuit?

Constructing circuits and drawing circuit diagrams

An **electric circuit** is a complete path around which an **electric current** can flow. A circuit contains:

- a cell or a battery of cells
- at least one device that can transfer energy, e.g. a lamp
- wires, called connecting leads, which join the cell to the components in the circuit
- a switch (usually included).

The table shows the symbols for frequently used components.

Below is a circuit and circuit diagram:

- The components can be identified using the table.
- The arrows represent the electric current flowing round the circuit.
- The **ammeter** measures the size of the electric current.

> The unit for electric current is the **ampere**, usually abbreviated to amp (**A**).

cell	battery	lamp
—┤├—	—┤├⋯┤├—	—⊗—
resistor	**open switch**	**closed switch**
—▭—	—⌒ ∘—	—∘∘—
ammeter	**voltmeter**	**variable resistor**
—(A)—	—(V)—	—⫻—

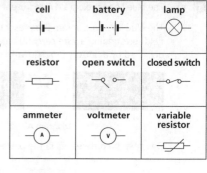

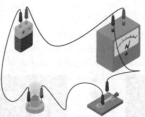

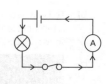

Series and parallel circuits

A **series circuit** has just one route for electric current to flow. One switch controls the whole circuit. The lamps are either both on, or both off. The current value is the same all around the circuit. The current leaving the cell is equal to the current returning to the cell.	
In a **parallel circuit** there are two or more branches around which electric current can flow. The lamps can be switched on and off separately. The current leaving the cell splits, so some flows through each lamp. The two currents then recombine and return to the cell.	

This circuit contains a resistor and a lamp connected in series. Energy from the cell is transferred to the surroundings by both the resistor and the lamp. The voltmeter is connected in parallel with the resistor. It gives information about the energy transferred by the resistor. The name given to the quantity being measured is **potential difference** (also known as voltage).

All electrical components try to oppose the flow of current to some extent. **Resistance** is a measure of this. The resistor is a component designed to have a specific amount of resistance. It is used in complex circuits to control the size of the current. You can find the resistance of the resistor by dividing the voltmeter reading by the ammeter reading.

> The unit of potential difference is the **volt** (V). The unit of resistance is the **ohm** (Ω).

What is an electric circuit?

Constructing circuits and drawing circuit diagrams

1. In the space provided, draw the circuit diagram for the circuit shown below.

Series and parallel circuits

2. The symbol for a cell has a longer line and a shorter line. The longer line is the positive terminal. The shorter line is the negative terminal. Look at the circuit below.

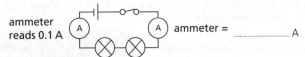

ammeter reads 0.1 A   ammeter = _____ A

a) Are the lamps connected in series or in parallel? _____

b) Add an arrow to the circuit diagram to show the current direction between the lamps.

c) Add the current reading in the space provided next to the circuit diagram.

3. In the circuit below, two lamps are connected to a cell. The ammeters, X, Y, and Z, measure the current flowing at different points in the circuit.

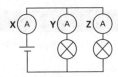

a) Are the lamps connected in series or in parallel? _____

b) Draw an arrow on the circuit to show the direction of the current as it leaves the cell.

c) i) Tick the correct box to show which ammeter has the highest reading.

    X ☐   Y ☐   Z ☐

   ii) Explain your answer.

   _____

   _____

   _____

How can we investigate electrical resistance in a circuit?

Measuring resistance

Resistance, for example the resistance of a metal wire, can be measured:

- A 1-metre length of wire is cut from the spool and connected into the circuit as shown, with an ammeter to measure the current through the wire.
- A voltmeter is connected across the wire to measure the potential difference.
- To calculate the wire's resistance, use the equation:
  resistance = potential difference ÷ current

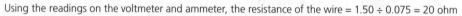

wire

Using the readings on the voltmeter and ammeter, the resistance of the wire = 1.50 ÷ 0.075 = 20 ohm

> To calculate resistance, divide the voltmeter reading by the ammeter reading.

Investigating a factor that affects resistance

A wire's resistance depends on its length, its thickness and the material from which it is made.

When investigating how the wire's thickness affects its resistance, the thickness is the **independent variable**. The wire's resistance is the **dependent variable**.

The other factors (the wire's length and material) must not change during the experiment. So, these are the **control variables**.

The above circuit is used to measure the resistance of 1 metre lengths of wire from five different spools. The spools have wire of the same material but different thicknesses. The results are shown in the table. There is a pattern in the data so we can conclude that a thicker wire has a smaller resistance.

> Recording data in order in a table helps with spotting a pattern.

Thickness in mm	Resistance in ohms
0.21	32
0.27	20
0.31	15
0.35	12
0.40	9

Using the particle model to explain resistance

Metal particles inside the metal wire are arranged in rows. Free electrons move around randomly inside the metal.

- When a cell is connected across the wire, the electrons drift in one direction creating an electric current.
- Each time electrons collide with particles they lose some kinetic energy.
- The cell has to supply more energy to keep the electrons drifting one way.

A gap between two rows of particles is an 'easy path' for the drifting electrons. The thicker the wire, the greater the number of 'easy paths'. So, less energy is needed to maintain the electron flow, and so the resistance is smaller.

metal particle   electron

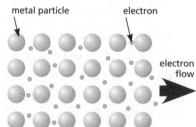

electron flow

> It takes more energy to keep an electric current flowing through a component with a high resistance than one with a low resistance.

How can we investigate electrical resistance in a circuit?

Measuring resistance

1 A student is using this circuit to check the value of a resistor.

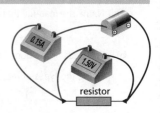

a) Give the name of the meter that measures electric current.

....

b) Give the name of the meter that measures potential difference.

....

resistor

c) The student measures the current and potential difference for the resistor. Use the meter readings to calculate the resistance of the resistor. .... ohm

Investigating a factor that affects resistance

2 Two factors that affect the resistance of nichrome wire are its length and its thickness. A student uses this circuit to investigate how the resistance of the wire depends on its length, measured with a metre rule.

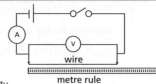

wire
metre rule

a) Draw lines to match each type of variable to the correct quantity.

dependent variable		thickness
independent variable		resistance
control variable		length

b) Describe how you would use the circuit to measure the resistance of a length of the wire.

....

c) The table shows the student's results.

What pattern does the student's data show?

Length in cm	20	40	60	80	100
Resistance in ohms	6	13	19	26	32

Using the particle model to explain resistance

3 When a wire is connected to a battery, electrons drift along through the wire creating an electric current. The electrons lose energy when they collide with the metal particles in the wire. The battery has to continue supplying energy to keep the electrons drifting along.

Circle the correct options to complete the sentences.

Electrons moving through a longer wire will have **more/fewer** collisions than in a shorter wire. So a

longer wire would require **more/less** energy to keep the electrons drifting along. And so a longer

wire has **more/less** resistance.

Mixed questions

1 Look at the diagram of the femur bone from a person's leg.

  a) Name the material that coats the end of the bones at A and B.

      ....

  b) The ends of the bone form joints.

      Name the types of moveable joint found at **A** and at **B**.

      A ....

      B ....

  c) What tissue connects muscles to this bone?

      ....

  d) The length of this bone is 50 cm.

      Use this equation to estimate the height of the person:

      height of the person = (length of the femur × 2.6) + 65

      ....

2 A student measures the sides of a wooden block. He measures the mass of the block using a balance.

Mass of block = 1.6 kg

  a) Gravitational field strength at the Earth's surface is 10 N/kg.

      i) Calculate the weight of the block. .... N

      ii) The block is on a bench in the position shown.
         Calculate the area of the block in contact with the bench. .... m²

      iii) The block exerts a contact force on the bench equal to its weight.
          Calculate the pressure exerted by the block on the bench.

          Use the equation: **pressure = force ÷ area**

          .... newton per square metre

  b) The student puts the wooden block into a tank of water to
      see if it floats. The red arrows show the pressure exerted by
      the water on the wooden block.

      i) What causes a liquid to exert pressure on an object?

         ....

      ii) The pressure due to the liquid on the vertical sides of the block acts in opposite directions
         and so cancels the effect. What is the name given to the force created by liquid pressure
         on the underside of the block?

         ....

      iii) The student observes that the block of wood floats in the water. What does this tell you
         about the block's weight and the force on the underside of the block?

         ....

iv) What does the observation that the block floats tell you about how densely packed the matter is in the wood compared with water?

....

c) The student is given a solid block of steel. The matter in steel is packed 7 times more densely than water.

i) Would a solid block of steel float or sink if placed in the water tank? ....

ii) The student knows that the hull of some ships is made of steel. She gets a baking tray made of steel and places it on the water in the tank.
Explain why the steel baking tray floats.

baking tray

....

....

....

3 Fermentation happens in yeast.

a) Describe what is meant by fermentation.

....

....

b) A student decides to investigate the effect of temperature on the rate of fermentation by yeast.

Write **one** way that the student could measure the rate of fermentation.

....

c) Write the independent variable in the student's experiment.

....

4 The diagram shows the alloy brass. Brass is an alloy of mainly copper and 40% zinc.

a) Add labels to name the two elements in the diagram.

i) →

ii) →

i) .... **ii)** ....

b) What percentage of brass is made of copper? ....

c) Explain why brass is stronger than pure copper.

....

....

d) Brass can react with nitric acid. Name the gas that is produced in this reaction.

....

e) Zinc can react with hydrochloric acid but brass cannot. Complete the word equation for the reaction between zinc and hydrochloric acid.

.... + ... → .... + ...

Mixed questions

5 The diagram shows a plant cell from a leaf.

a) Which letter labels:

   i) the vacuole?

   ii) the site of photosynthesis?

   iii) the site of anaerobic respiration?

b) Complete the gaps in these sentences.

The structure in the diagram above labelled .... is only active during the day because

it needs ....

Structure B uses the gas .... because it is the site of aerobic respiration.

6 The diagram shows views of the lower epidermis from two types of plant, **X** and **Y**.

Plant X	Plant Y

a) Describe the main difference between the lower epidermis of the two plants.

....

b) One of the plants is adapted to live in a hot dry area.

Suggest which plant it is, giving a reason for your answer.

....

....

7 Natural gas is used in many homes for cooking and heating. This fuel is mainly made of methane gas.

a) Draw a particle model diagram of
methane gas in the space provided.

b) Explain why methane gas can be compressed.

....

....

c) Complete the word equation for the complete combustion of methane.

methane + ... → carbon dioxide + ...

8 A student builds a model of a scrap yard crane designed to pick up objects made of magnetic material. She uses an iron rod and copper wire insulated with green plastic.

The iron rod can be raised or lowered by adjusting the position of the clamp. When the wire is connected to the cell, the iron rod becomes magnetised.

a) Is the magnetism in the rod temporary or permanent?

....

b) The student lowers the iron rod into a dish containing paperclips. Some are made of copper, some plastic, and some steel. Which type of paperclip would become attached to the iron rod?

c) What does the student do to make the crane release the paperclip?

....

9 Look at the diagram of a food web.

a) What is the trophic level of the rabbit?

....

b) Write out a food chain from this web that has four organisms.

....

c) A gardener uses a toxic chemical that kills mice.

Explain what effect this might have on the numbers of these animals:

owls: ....

....

shrews: ....

....

10 The cell drives an electric current around the circuit shown.

a) Which way does the current flow through the resistor? Tick the correct box.

from right to left ☐   from left to right ☐

b) The ammeter reads 0.25 A. The voltmeter reads 1.5 V.

Calculate the resistance of the resistor. .... ohm

Scientific skills

What are the different types of scientific investigation?

Types of research

Scientists ask questions. Using the knowledge they already have, scientists have ideas about what the answers to the questions might be. To test these ideas, scientists carry out **scientific investigations**, in which they collect **data**.

There are two main types of investigation:
- **primary research** – where you collect the data first hand
- **secondary research** – where you use data that other people have collected like those found in books, trusted internet sites and data your teacher has collected.

For primary research you could complete:
- **an experiment**, where you change the independent variable and collect data on the change observed in the dependent variable, e.g. the time it takes for 0.1 g of magnesium to fully react with different concentrations of hydrochloric acid
- **a survey**, where you monitor something that is already happening, e.g. the number of minutes of daylight in a certain day.

In a scientific experiment, the research tries to find out the relationship between the **independent variable** and the **dependent variable**.

During an experiment, the data is collected and recorded into a results table. This should be drawn in advance so that only the dependent variable results are written down during the investigation.

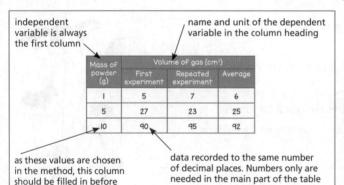

independent variable is always the first column

name and unit of the dependent variable in the column heading

Mass of powder (g)	Volume of gas (cm³)		
	First experiment	Repeated experiment	Average
1	5	7	6
5	27	23	25
10	90	95	92

as these values are chosen in the method, this column should be filled in before the investigation starts

data recorded to the same number of decimal places. Numbers only are needed in the main part of the table as the units are in the column heading

Researchers must keep all the other control variables the same to make the data valid. Valid data is information that can be used to find out if the scientist's idea that is being investigated is correct or incorrect.

In a scientific survey, it is often useful to collect the data in a **frequency table (tally chart)**. This is a quick way to keep track of what is being observed.

Favourite Fruit

FRUIT	TALLY
Orange	ⵜⵜⵜ ⵜⵜⵜ I
Apple	ⵜⵜⵜ ⵜⵜⵜ
Banana	ⵜⵜⵜ III
Strawberry	ⵜⵜⵜ II
Pineapple	IIII

Scientific skills

How is data recorded?

Units

Units are used so that measurements can be compared. There are **quantities** that are often measured in science and you need to know their standard units:

Variable	Unit	Symbol
time	seconds	s
length	metres	m
mass	grams	g
volume	cubic centimetres	cm³
speed	metres per second	m/s
density	grams per cubic centimetre	g/cm³
force	newton	N

Prefixes

In science, we often work with numbers that are very big or very small. **Prefixes** can be used to make the numbers more manageable and scientists change the units so that the number is between 1 and 100.

Think about a common variable that you might measure and how you could use the prefixes to change the unit by a factor of ten.

Some examples you are likely to come across include:
- a **kilo**gram is one thousand **grams**
- a **centi**metre is one hundredth of a **metre**
- a **milli**litre is a thousandth of a **litre**.

> Prefixes are used when you get data for your mobile phone or internet. Data transfer is measured in units of byte (B) but we transfer so much data now that you probably have a package measured in gigabytes (1,000,000,000 bytes) or terabytes (1,000,000,000,000 bytes)!

Time

In investigations, stopwatches or timers are often used to measure time.

Consider a stopwatch that displays 1:30; we read this as 1 minute and 30 seconds, but this is actually two units. So the value needs to be converted either into 90 seconds or 1.5 minutes. (It should never be written as '1.30 minutes', which is actually 78 seconds!)

Scientific skills

What is a chart?

Data from investigations need to be interpreted to find **patterns** and draw **conclusions**. It can be difficult to notice patterns when you are looking at raw data in a table, so mathematical representations like **charts** can be used to help you see patterns more clearly.

To choose what kind of chart to use, you need to think about the type of data that your dependent and independent variables are. Data can be:
- **categoric** – described as a word, e.g. eye colour
- **discrete** – a specific number, e.g. shoe size; you can be a whole size or half size but nothing in between
- **continuous** – any number in a given range, e.g. the temperature of a room.

Bar charts

Bar charts usually have:
- the independent variable on the x-axis, which is either categoric or discrete
- the dependent variable on the y-axis, which is discrete or continuous
- the height of the bars representing the frequency.

> When drawing a bar chart, always have a suitable scale on the x-axis and a suitable scale on the y-axis. Make sure both axes are labelled.
> Draw the bars accurately and neatly using a ruler.

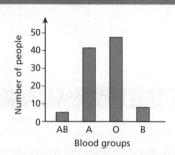

Pie charts

Pie charts show the proportion of each group as part of the area of a circle. Pie charts usually have:
- an independent variable that is categoric or discrete
- a dependent variable that can be represented as a ratio or percentage
- the angle of each group representing the fraction (out of 360) for that data value
- each group labelled either directly on the pie chart or by a colour code key.

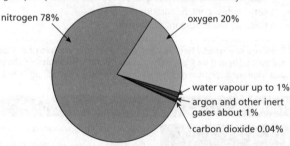

> When drawing a pie chart, you need to work out the fraction of the total that each section represents. Use a protractor for this.

Venn diagrams

Venn diagrams are a mathematical representation which allow you to compare the features of different groups and consider their relationship to each other. Each group has a circle. Information for each group is placed in their circle and any features shared by more than one group is written in the overlap between their circles.

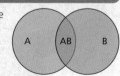

Scientific skills

What is a graph?

A **graph** is a type of chart that looks at the numerical relationship between two numerical quantities. In a graph:
- both variables are continuous
- the independent variable is plotted on the x-axis
- the dependent variable is plotted on the y-axis

When plotting a graph, choose scales carefully so that the data is plotted over at least half of the graph paper. This makes it easier to spot any patterns.

Plot the points with crosses (x) and not dots (·) as this is more accurate. The size of the cross indicates your confidence in the measurement. So, the more confident you are, the smaller the cross should be.

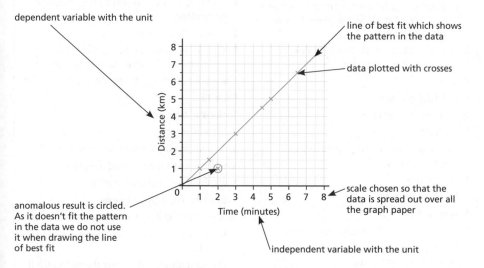

dependent variable with the unit

line of best fit which shows the pattern in the data

data plotted with crosses

scale chosen so that the data is spread out over all the graph paper

anomalous result is circled. As it doesn't fit the pattern in the data we do not use it when drawing the line of best fit

independent variable with the unit

The point of a graph is to see a pattern in the data and to make **predictions**. If there are some points that do not fit the pattern, circle them: these are called **anomalous points**. So, hold your graph at arm's length and look at the points:
- Do they form a straight line? Use a ruler to draw a straight line of best fit going through as many of the points as you can.
- Do they form a curve? In a smooth arc, try to draw a curve with just one stroke of the pencil.
- Do they form any pattern at all? If there is no pattern, do not draw a line of best fit.

Make sure that you use a sharp pencil and draw one clear **line of best fit**. It is important not to sketch or make a thick line, because the predictions that you make from these lines will be less useful.

> Line of best fit in maths means using a ruler to draw the trend line. But in science, line of best fit just means the line that shows the relationship between the independent and dependent variable. So, in science, lines of best fit can be straight lines, curves or even shapes.

Answers

Biology

1. a) cranium **b)** ribs **c)** femur **d)** ulna, radius

2. vertebrae

3. It makes blood cells.

4. They contain protein.

5. a) X-ray machine

   b) femur

   c) By making a plaster cast to hold the bones together so that they can repair themselves; By inserting metal pins or plates to hold the bones together.

6. Calcium makes the hard part of bone. Without it, the bone is too flexible.

Page 7

1. a) A **b)** D **c)** C **d)** B

2. a ball and socket joint

3. a) cartilage

   b) to absorb shock and stop the bones rubbing together

4. a) ligaments

   b) to absorb shock

5. synovial fluid

6. The cartilage on the bones wears away.

7. The metal must be hardwearing/strong/ unreactive/must not rust.

Page 9

1. the heart

2. to connect muscles to bones

3. nerve messages from the brain

4. They act as pivots.

5. a) i) C **ii)** B

   b) The arm would straighten (extend).

6. antagonistic muscles

7. Muscles can only contract to pull on bones; they cannot push.

8. 100N

9. to increase their muscle strength

Page 11

1. muscle contraction

2. amino acids

3. to allow the cardiac muscle to contract so that it pumps blood

4. glucose + oxygen → carbon dioxide + water

5. Oxygen is taken in from air in the lungs and is transported to body cells by the blood.

6. Energy is **released** in cells by the process of **respiration**.

7. water, carbon dioxide

8. a) inner membrane: is folded to increase the surface area for respiration to take place

   b) matrix: contains the enzymes for respiration

Page 13

1. glucose, oxygen

2. the sun/sunlight

3. carbon dioxide; stomata; soil; xylem vessels

4. to transport sugars around the plant

5. a) during the day/when it is light

   b) all the time/day and night

6. a) to kill the leaf and remove the green colour

   b) Ethanol could catch fire if there is a naked flame nearby.

   c) Pour **iodine** solution over the leaf and, if it turns **black**, starch is present.

Page 15

1. the heart

2. artery

3. vein

4. small intestine

5. salivary glands

6. trachea, bronchi, bronchioles

7. glucose; oxygen; alveoli; carbon dioxide

8. Less air can reach the alveoli so less oxygen is absorbed into the bloodstream, leading to a decrease in respiration in cells.

Answers

Page 17

1.

	Aerobic respiration	Anaerobic respiration
Does it use oxygen?	✓	✗
Does it use glucose?	✓	✓
Does it make lactic acid?	✗	✓
Does it happen in mitochondria?	✓	✗

2. Enzymes are protein molecules that speed up the rate of biological reactions.

3. glucose → ethanol + carbon dioxide + energy released

4. fermentation; carbon dioxide

5. It turns it milky.

6. a) to stop oxygen getting to the mixture so respiration is anaerobic

   b) The bubbles may be different sizes/It is possible to miscount the bubbles.

Page 19

1. wood

2. to supply oxygen/to supply food/to supply fuel/to remove carbon dioxide from the air/ for medical drugs/for decoration in homes and gardens

3. They can make their own food.

4. It can result in less oxygen in the atmosphere and increased concentration of carbon dioxide.

5. chemical reactions

6. in the soil; around hydrothermal vents

7. a) true **b)** true **c)** false **d)** false **e)** false **f)** true

Page 21

1. carbon dioxide, water

2. The animal made carbon dioxide for the plant to use in photosynthesis and the plant made oxygen for the animal to use in respiration.

3. chloroplasts; cytoplasm

4. a) B **b)** C **c)** D

5. to make cell walls

6. growth

Page 23

1. a) at night/when it is dark

   b) They cannot photosynthesise in the dark so do not need carbon dioxide.

2. they shrink

3. 15 stomata in 0.1 mm², so in 1 mm² there are 150

4. brightness of the light, carbon dioxide concentration

5. Count the number of bubbles of oxygen given off in one minute.

6. a) temperature

   b) 20°C

   c) so that the light intensity/brightness is the same as this would affect photosynthesis

Page 25

1. transpiration

2. xylem; pulled; lignin; one

3. They increase the surface area of roots to absorb water and minerals.

4. carbon, hydrogen, oxygen

5. They cannot make chlorophyll.

6. Proteins contain nitrogen and the sugars made by photosynthesis do not.

7. a) potassium

   b) 15 kg

   c) Manure needs to be decomposed first to release the minerals but artificial fertiliser has the minerals ready to be absorbed by plants.

Page 27

1. a) trophic level **b)** producers **c)** primary consumers; plant **d)** animals

2. a) seaweed, phytoplankton

   b) lobsters, sea urchins

   c) four

   d) They hunt and kill fish and lobsters to eat.

   e) three

3. respiration/movement/keeping warm

4. As energy is lost at each trophic level, there is not enough energy left.

Answers

Page 29

1. Interdependence – When two organisms rely on each other for resources

   Equilibrium – When the numbers of predators and prey are constant

   Predator–prey graph – A chart showing how the numbers of predators and prey change

2. **a)** lynx

   b) Lynx numbers increased, so they ate more hares. This caused hare numbers to drop, therefore there was less food available for lynx so their numbers fell. This allowed hare numbers to increase.

3. poisonous chemicals

4. Pesticides are used by farmers to kill weeds or insects and can be taken in by small organisms/washed into rivers and reservoirs.

5. The pesticide may be taken in by a prey organism and not broken down. This means that the pesticide will build up in predators, as they eat more and more prey.

Chemistry

Page 31

1. **a)** false **b)** false **c)** true **d)** true **e)** true

2. **a)** Intermolecular forces are too strong to let the particles move past each other.

   b)

   c) random and in all directions

3. Liquid mixture – More than one colour of particle, particles are still touching but not a regular arrangement

   Gaseous alcohol – One colour of particle, particles not touching and in a random arrangement

   Liquid alcohol – One colour of particle, particles are still touching but not a regular arrangement

Page 33

1. **a)** sublimation **b)** evaporation/boiling **c)** condensation **d)** solidifying/freezing

2. **a)** 0°C **b)** 100°C

3. Substances must always melt before they can boil. So, the melting point must always be at a lower temperature than the boiling point.

4. Melting point – The temperature at which a pure substance changes from being a solid to a liquid

   Boiling point – The temperature at which a pure substance changes from being a liquid to a gas

   Latent heat – The energy used to overcome intermolecular forces to change state

5. **a)** and **c)**

Page 35

1. **a)** the random movement of particles in a fluid (liquid or gas)

   b) liquid, gas

2. Cooking oil has weaker intermolecular forces of attraction between its particles compared to honey. So, the cooking oil particles can move and slide over each other more easily than the honey particles, making it less viscous.

3. increase the temperature; decrease the volume; add more particles

4. **a)** expansion **b)** compression **c)** expansion **d)** compression

5. Solubility decreases with increasing temperature.

6. The intermolecular force of attraction between the gas particle and the solvent particle is greater than the intermolecular force of attraction between all the gas particles.

Page 37

1. gas

2. top pan balance

3. cm^3 (or: $m^3/dm^3/l/ml$)

4. **a)** density = mass ÷ volume

   b) density = mass ÷ volume = 27 ÷ 10 = 2.7 g/cm^3

Answers

5. a) Floats: cooking oil; Sinks: water

b) Floats: water; Sinks: syrup

c) Floats: cooking oil; Sinks: syrup

d) Floats: water; Sinks: polystyrene foam

e) Floats: cooking oil; Sinks: polystyrene foam

f) Floats: polystyrene foam; Sinks: syrup

Page 39

1. a) true **b)** false **c)** false **d)** false

2. 231.2 g

3. 24.5 g

4. 0.0025 g/cm³

5. 50%

6. add water

7. An increase in concentration means there are more gas particles in the same space. So, there are more collisions with the container and so a higher pressure.

Page 41

1. a) false **b)** true **c)** true **d)** true **e)** true

2.

3. increase the concentration gradient; increase the temperature

4. -273°C

5. gas

Page 43

1. copper and tin

2. They contain more than one element/ substance not chemically joined.

3. They are sonorous/lustrous/conductors/ malleable/ductile.

4. It is cheaper/stronger/more hard wearing.

5. The carbon atoms make it more difficult for the layers of iron atoms to slide over each other.

6. Foam – A mixture of gas bubbles trapped inside a liquid; Emulsion – A mixture of two liquids (one water-based, the other oil-based) that do not normally mix; Aerosol – A mixture of particles of liquid or solid dispersed in a gas; Gel – A mixture of liquid particles floating in a solid

Page 45

1. a) alkali

b) alkali

c) acid

d) alkali

2. pH greater than 7 – alkali

pH equal to 7 – neutral

pH less than 7 – acid

3. acidity

4. a) red

b) purple

5. a) acid

b) Purple/blue/dark green because it is a cleaning spray and cleaning products are alkali.

Page 47

1. a change where a new substance is made

2. A gas/new substance was made. This is a chemical reaction.

3. acid; neutral; wasp; vinegar

4. Add a base/alkali to the vinegar.

5. Universal indicator

6. nitric acid – metal nitrate; hydrochloric acid – metal chloride; sulfuric acid – metal sulfate

7. to make glass

Page 49

1. zinc chloride and hydrogen

2. calcium + sulfuric acid → calcium sulfate + hydrogen

3. Hold a lit splint in the gas and listen for a (squeaky) pop.

4. sodium chloride, carbon dioxide and water

5. calcium + hydrochloric acid → calcium chloride + carbon dioxide + water

6. Blow through limewater and watch to see if it turns from colourless to cloudy.

7. magnesium chloride; water

Answers

8. copper oxide + sulfuric acid → copper sulfate + water

9. potassium nitrate and water

10. sodium hydroxide + sulfuric acid → sodium sulfate + water

Page 51

1. oxygen

2. exothermic

3. fuel, oxygen and heat

4. It smothers the fire, removing the oxygen.

5. hydrogen and carbon

6. a) propane + oxygen → carbon dioxide + water

   b) oxygen + ethane → carbon dioxide + carbon + carbon monoxide + water

7. carbon dioxide – global climate change; carbon (soot) – respiratory problems and global dimming; carbon monoxide – toxic gas; oxides of sulfur and nitrogen – acid rain

Physics

Page 53

1. a) negative

   b) electric field

   c) non-contact force

2. a) positive

   b) repulsive force; the rods have the same type of charge

3. a) It is more spread out.

   b) The positively charged paint droplets from the electrostatic gun exert a repulsive force on each other. This pushes the charged droplets further apart.

Page 55

1. a) the gravitational force on a mass of 1 kg

   b) g

   c) newton per kilogram or N/kg

2. a) W = mg

   b) weight W = mg = 80 × 10 = 800 N

3. It decreases.

4. force of gravity = weight = mg = 1000 × 3.7 = 3700 N

5. a) It decreases. b) It increases.

   c) Two horizontal arrows of the same length on the spacecraft, one pointing towards the Earth, the other towards the Moon.

   d) the Sun

Page 57

1. a) i) weight

      ii) area = width × length

   b) contact force exerted on table = 200 N. area of box in contact with table = (0.4 × 0.5) = 0.2 m²

   c) pressure = (200 ÷ 0.2 =) 1000 N/m²

2. pressure = (10 ÷ 0.0000001 =) 100,000,000 N/m²

3. area of elephant's feet = 4 × 0.2 = 0.8 m² pressure = 30,000 ÷ 0.8 = 37,500 N/m²

4. The force exerted by the tank on the ground is spread over the tank's tracks. The tracks have a very large area.

Page 59

1. a) The liquid particles are always moving around and bumping into each other.

   b) particles are very close together; particles are not arranged in a pattern

2. There is greater weight of liquid above level Y than above level X.

3. a) Liquid pressure on the bottom of the dam is greater.

   b) longer horizontal arrow at a greater depth in the water, pointing to the right with arrowhead close to dam wall

4. a) B

   b) upthrust

   c) The block in B is fully submerged so more liquid is displaced.

Page 61

1. a) Gas particles are moving around very quickly.

   b) large gaps between particles; particles are not arranged in a pattern

2. Gas particles collide with the surface.

Answers

3. the Earth's gravitational field/gravity

4. At sea level, the gaps between the molecules are smaller.

5. a) $80,000\,N/m^2$

   b) lack of oxygen

   c) i) 4000 m

   ii) a change in the weather

Page 63

1. iron/nickel/steel/cobalt/neodymium

2. map reading/navigating a ship

3. the head

4. to the Earth's North Pole

5.

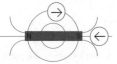

6. a) moves to the right/attracted to the magnet

   b) moves to the left/repelled by the magnet

   c) has no effect

Page 65

1. a magnet that retains its magnetism

2. iron/nickel/cobalt/neodymium

3. a) magnet b) domain; fields c) domains

4. electromagnet

5. a) solenoid

   b) Connect it to a battery.

   c) Place an iron core inside the coil.

   d) Disconnect the battery.

6. a) permanent; strong field

   b) temporary; weak field

   c) temporary; strong field

Page 67

1. a) a coil (with iron core)

   b) a magnetic field

   c) An electromagnet can be switched on and off./The strength of the electromagnet can be varied.

2. a) and b)

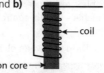

   c) The core becomes magnetised.

   d) The end of the iron plate moves towards the core. Switch 2 is closed. The spring is stretched.

   e) It is safer.

Page 69

1. a) Diagram A: The field lines are straight and equally spaced. Diagram B: The field lines are circular and are not equally spaced.

   b) A magnetic field is strongest where field lines are closer together.

2. a) On the left of the coil: arrow downwards. On the right of the coil: arrow upwards.

   b) Swap round the connections to the cell.

   c) The coil is moving.

Page 71

1.

2. a) series

   b) arrow drawn from the right pointing to the left

   c) 0.1 A

3. a) parallel

   b) arrow drawn pointing upwards from the longer line of the cell symbol

   c) i) X

   ii) The current through X splits to go through Y and Z so X must have the highest reading.

Page 73

1. a) ammeter

   b) voltmeter

   c) resistance = (1.5 ÷ 0.15 =) 10 ohm

Answers

2. a) dependent variable – resistance; independent variable – length; control variable – thickness

b) Close the switch. Divide the voltmeter reading by the ammeter reading.

c) The longer the length, the greater the resistance.

3. more; more; more

Mixed questions

Pages 74–77

1. a) cartilage

b) A = ball and socket

B = hinge

c) ligaments

d) (50 × 2.6) + 65 = 195 cm

2. a) i) weight = (1.6 × 10 =) 16 N

ii) area = (0.2 × 0.1 =) 0.02 m²

iii) pressure = (16 ÷ 0.02 =) 800 newton per square metre

b) i) Liquid particles can move around and bombard the surface of the object.

ii) upthrust

iii) They are equal/balanced.

iv) The wood is less densely packed than water.

c) i) sink

ii) The area of the underside of the tray in contact with the water is large, so the upthrust created is large and can support the tray's weight.

3. a) anaerobic respiration that makes ethanol and carbon dioxide

b) Collect and measure/count the bubbles of carbon dioxide given off.

c) temperature

4. a) i) copper **ii)** zinc

b) 60%

c) The zinc atoms are bigger than the copper atoms and prevent the layers of metal atoms sliding as easily.

d) hydrogen

e) zinc + hydrochloric acid → zinc chloride + hydrogen

5. a) i) C **ii)** A **iii)** D

b) A; sunlight; oxygen

6. a) Plant X has more stomata.

b) Plant Y because it has fewer stomata so will lose less water.

7. a)

b) There is a lot of space between the gas particles so when they are squeezed, they can move closer together easily and the material takes up less space, but the particles themselves do not change size.

c) methane + oxygen → carbon dioxide + water

8. a) temporary

b) steel paperclips

c) disconnects a wire from the cell

9. a) primary consumer

b) leaf litter → worm → shrew → owl

c) owls: Numbers might fall as they have less food to eat/due to bioaccumulation of the toxic chemical.

shrews: Numbers might fall as owls will eat more of them.

10. a) from right to left

b) Resistance = (1.5 ÷ 0.25 =) 6 ohm